D1044591

World's Worst
WEAPONS

Exploding Tanks, Uncontrollable Ships, and Unflyable Aircraft

Martin J. Dougherty

amber
BOOKS

World's Worst
WEAPONS

Exploding Tanks, Uncontrollable Ships and Unflyable Aircraft

Martin J. Dougherty

amber
BOOKS

Reprinted in 2017, 2018

This edition published in 2016

Copyright © 2016 Amber Books Ltd

All rights reserved. No part of this publication may be reproduced, stored in a retrieval system, or transmitted in any form or by any means, electronic, mechanical, photocopying, recording, or otherwise, without prior written permission of the copyright holder.

Published by
Amber Books Ltd
United House
North Road
London N7 9DP
United Kingdom
www.amberbooks.co.uk
Instagram: amberbooksltd
Facebook: www.facebook.com/amberbooks
Twitter: @amberbooks

ISBN: 978-1-78274-364-4

Project Editor: James Bennett
Design: Tony Cohen
Picture Research: Terry Forshaw

Printed in China

CONTENTS

INTRODUCTION

E arly humans, possessing a fairly puny set of natural weapons, discovered that they could hunt, fend off predators and compete with one another more effectively if they made tools to help with the job. The prize for the individual or group with the best weapons was survival, prosperity, and dominance. The arms race that began with sharp sticks is still going on today.

Some weapons are easy to use, powerful, effective, reliable, accurate… the list of possible accolades is lengthy. This book is about the others, the weapons that really should never have been made. Poor design and implementation, flawed concepts or technology that simply did not come up to scratch, too many design compromises – any of these factors can result in a weapon that few people would want to use and nobody should have to depend on.

Some bad weapons are virtually useless. Others seem to be unfortunate, in that they are based on an intelligent concept but ended up being used in the wrong place in the wrong time. Then there are a few cases of weapons that are simply not that good, but have some redeeming feature which make them useful, or have managed to be a success despite their many flaws. The weapons in this book cover all these categories, but also includes those gems which were based on terrible ideas, didn't work, and had no redeeming features at all.

Above: The Bachem Natter, a frighteningly makeshift rocket-powered interceptor.
Right: The Tiger I tank was feared by the Allies, but had an inadequate engine and its tracks were prone to clogging with mud.

PERSONAL AND INFANTRY WEAPONS

For as long as human beings have been fighting one another over territory, resources or ideology, the mainstay of any conflict has been the man, usually fighting on foot, armed with an effective personal weapon. There have, however, been exceptions. Some very poor weapons were issued for lack of anything better, or because they were not expected to be necessary. Some artillery crews in the American Civil War were issued a shortsword similar to the Roman gladius for self-defence purposes. It turned out to be a fairly useless impediment, and many were simply 'lost' on the march. Few saw use, and in truth the issuers probably never really intended them to.

Other mediocre and downright bad weapons have been issued for political reasons or because something much better was in the pipeline but not yet available. Some were simply outdated at the time they came into use. Years before, they were effective weapons but retirement was long overdue and the troops trying to use these weapons in combat found out why – the hard way.

Left: *This martial artist's skill with nunchaku was undoubtedly bought at the price of many self-inflicted injuries.*

NUNCHAKU (NUNCHUCKS) *TRADITIONAL*

Derived from an Asian farmer's tool and a favourite of martial arts fans, nunchaku consist of a pair of hardwood handles connected by a cord or short chain. They can be used to perform a range of impressive and complex techniques; however, they require great skill to handle properly and are most often a liability rather than an asset. Most people who try to use nunchaku end up hitting themselves.

The only reason that nunchaku were ever adopted as weapons was that the owners had nothing else. Possession of real weapons was punishable by death, so the subjugated farmers fought with what they had to hand.

SPECIFICATIONS

TYPE:	Personal hand to hand
LENGTH:	50–70cm (19–27in)
WEIGHT:	0.5kg (1lb)
RANGE:	Close combat
EASE OF USE:	Very low
COMPOSITION:	Wood and metal
USERS:	Japanese peasants, martial arts fans

Although they are great for impressing the public at displays, nunchaku are probably the flashiest and least effective of all martial arts weapons.

As well as being difficult and awkward weapons, nunchaku do not make particularly useful agricultural implements either.

Available in many kinds, nunchaku can also be improvised from a piece of cord and two lengths of wood.

11

THROWING STARS AND SHURIKEN *TRADITIONAL*

Made popular by the Ninja craze of the 1980s, these star-shaped throwing implements are wholly ineffective as weapons. Unless the pointed tips strike just right, a shuriken, or 'ninja star', will not cause any significant injury. Throwing them accurately is also problematical – most people could not hit a target with any part of the star, let alone a point.

When shuriken were used at all, it was as a distraction rather than a viable combat weapon. The popular movie image of a black-clad Ninja dispatching hordes of enemies with well-placed throwing stars is simply fantasy.

SPECIFICATIONS

TYPE:	Thrown
LENGTH:	10cm (4in)
WEIGHT:	Negligible
RANGE:	5m (16ft)
EASE OF USE:	Low
COMPOSITION:	Steel; can be crudely formed
USERS:	Martial arts fantasists

While fairly impressive in appearance, this large shuriken would cause a superficial (if painful) injury at best. Throwing it at an armoured Samurai would be an exercise in futility, and might merely serve to annoy him into a rather more effective response.

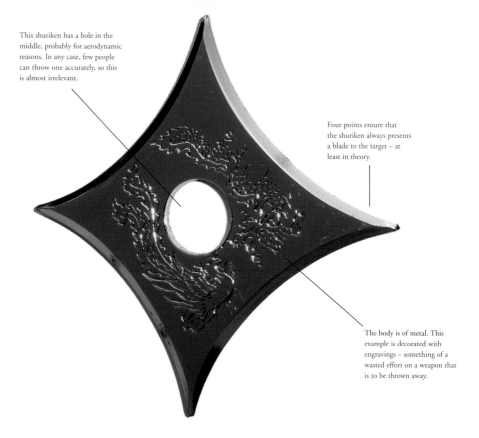

This shuriken has a hole in the middle, probably for aerodynamic reasons. In any case, few people can throw one accurately, so this is almost irrelevant.

Four points ensure that the shuriken always presents a blade to the target – at least in theory.

The body is of metal. This example is decorated with engravings – something of a wasted effort on a weapon that is to be thrown away.

SABRE-BRIQUET *1780*

The sabre-briquet was a light sword carried by French infantry in addition to the musket and bayonet. Usually having a curved slashing blade, various patterns were issued to Napoleonic infantry, and few were any use.

Fighting at close quarters, soldiers found they were better off with their bayonets or fighting with clubbed (reversed) muskets. Orders were given for the sabre-briquet to be abandoned in 1807, but as late as 1815 some regiments were still carrying their weapons. The best that can be said about the sabre-briquet was that it was sometimes useful for chopping firewood.

SPECIFICATIONS

TYPE:	Personal hand to hand
LENGTH:	1m (3ft)
WEIGHT:	1kg (2lb)
RANGE:	Close combat
EASE OF USE:	High
COMPOSITION:	Steel, often of poor quality
USERS:	Military

The real thing in action. Full-sized sabres as used by these French hussars were a deadly weapon in trained hands. The sabre-briquet was neither deadly nor placed in trained hands.

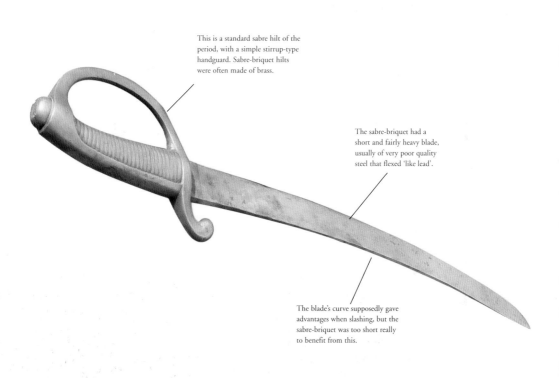

This is a standard sabre hilt of the period, with a simple stirrup-type handguard. Sabre-briquet hilts were often made of brass.

The sabre-briquet had a short and fairly heavy blade, usually of very poor quality steel that flexed 'like lead'.

The blade's curve supposedly gave advantages when slashing, but the sabre-briquet was too short really to benefit from this.

15

FLINTLOCK SWORD/PISTOLS *CIRCA 1800*

Another combination weapon that was tried from time to time was the combination sword/pistol. Essentially a fairly standard sword with a flintlock pistol mounted parallel to the blade and firing along it, the extra weight created an unwieldy sword and the pistol, even if it could be aimed and shot accurately, was of little use.

Flintlocks are awkward things to use and prone to misfire unless treated carefully. Waving a cocked pistol about is never a very good idea and clashing the weapon against an opponent's parry was likely to result in an accidental discharge – assuming of course that any powder remained in the pan.

SPECIFICATIONS

TYPE:	Personal
LENGTH:	1m (3ft)
WEIGHT:	1–1.5kg (2–3lb)
RANGE:	Close
EASE OF USE:	Low
COMPOSITION:	Steel, complex mechanism
USERS:	Private, self-defence

Pictured here is standard flintlock mechanism, using a spark created by flint striking steel. This would (hopefully) ignite a priming charge in the pan and set off the pistol. Flintlocks were notoriously unreliable.

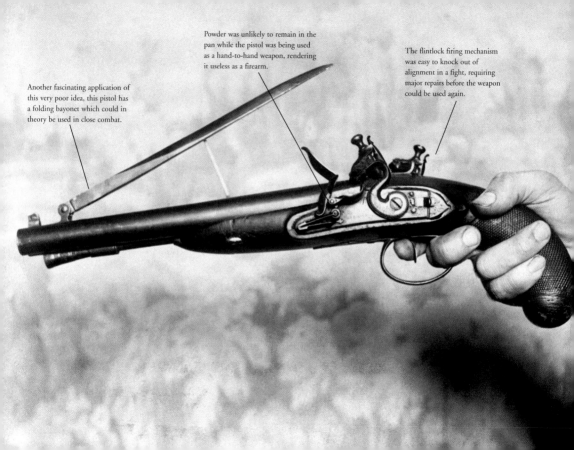

Another fascinating application of this very poor idea, this pistol has a folding bayonet which could in theory be used in close combat.

Powder was unlikely to remain in the pan while the pistol was being used as a hand-to-hand weapon, rendering it useless as a firearm.

The flintlock firing mechanism was easy to knock out of alignment in a fight, requiring major repairs before the weapon could be used again.

36 CALIBRE ADAMS REVOLVER 1851

The five-shot revolver patented by Robert Adams in 1851 was clever in concept but less effective in combat than the users would have liked. A cap-and-ball revolver that took a long time to load, the Adams was a double-action weapon, which was an advance on single-action weapons of the time.

The .36 version was decidedly ineffective. There were several cases of officers emptying their Adams into an enemy, then being bayoneted or sabred to death. Added to a tendency to burn the user's hands due to gas escaping around the cylinder, this made the Adams a somewhat dubious investment.

SPECIFICATIONS

TYPE:	Handgun
LENGTH:	25cm (9in)
CALIBRE:	.36
AMMUNITION CAPACITY:	5 rounds
EFFECTIVE RANGE:	40m (131ft)
COMPLEXITY:	Moderate
USERS:	Private, some military

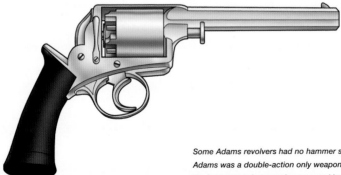

Some Adams revolvers had no hammer spur to allow thumb-cocking. The Adams was a double-action only weapon and thus did not need one. Note the large space between hammer and handgrip to allow hammer movement.

The Adams was an expensive item, and came to be considered a 'prestige' weapon after the Prince of Wales began to favour it. Many examples were heavily engraved and inlaid.

The overall lines of the Adams are quite modern. Many revolvers entering production a century later were quite similar in appearance.

The Adams was a well-balanced and very 'pointable' weapon. It was let down mainly by its lack of stopping power.

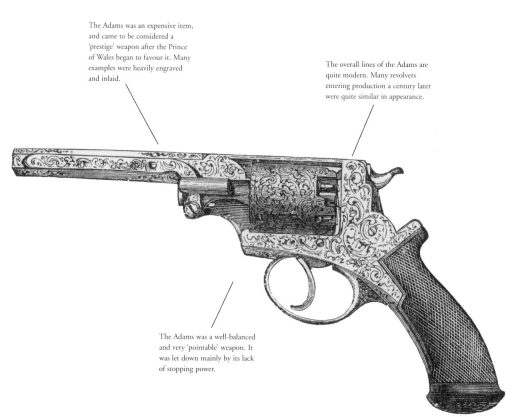

COLT REVOLVING CARBINE 1855

The 1855 Colt revolving carbine was an ingenious attempt to solve the problem of reloading for cavalrymen. Essentially a Colt cap-and-ball revolver with a stock and a carbine-length barrel, the concept was sound. The five-shot cylinder gave a man so armed a significant advantage over a trooper armed with a single-shot weapon.

It was not unknown, however, for the flash of one round being fired to ignite the other chambers. The result of a flashover was that one round went down the barrel and the others either exploded in the chamber or struck the weapon's frame and/or the user's hand.

SPECIFICATIONS

TYPE:	Longarm, cap and ball
LENGTH:	1.2m (4ft)
CALIBRE:	.45
AMMUNITION CAPACITY:	5 rounds
EFFECTIVE RANGE:	100m (328ft)
COMPLEXITY:	Moderate
USERS:	US Cavalry

The Colt's businesslike lines show an obvious relationship with long-barrelled Colt revolvers of the period. In many ways the carbine was simply an extended revolver.

Loading the cylinder with five rounds took time, but once loaded the Colt carbine offered greater firepower than the single-shot weapons in use elsewhere.

Although short by rifle standards, the extended carbine barrel gave a higher muzzle velocity and greater accuracy than a revolver.

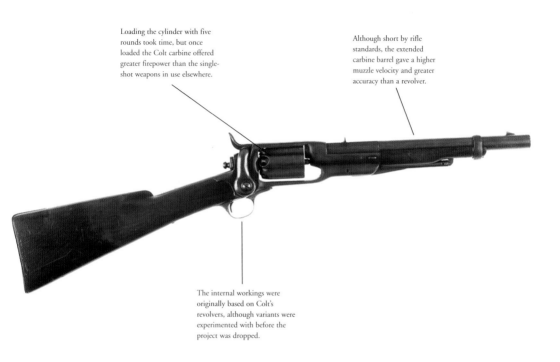

The internal workings were originally based on Colt's revolvers, although variants were experimented with before the project was dropped.

LE MAT GRAPESHOT REVOLVER *1856*

Designed from the outset as a cavalry weapon, the 'grapeshot' revolver gained its name from the inclusion of a shotgun cartridge in addition to the nine pistol rounds in its cylinder. A movable firing pin allowed the user to select between ammunition.

Although the legendary Confederate cavalry commander James 'Jeb' Stuart liked the weapon, it was a failure. Most of the examples of the Le Mat revolver that reached end users were badly made and tended to malfunction even if the user did not get himself into trouble by fiddling about with the firing pin in the middle of a firefight.

SPECIFICATIONS

TYPE:	Handgun
LENGTH:	25cm (9in)
CALIBRE:	Various. Initially .40 with a .60 shotgun cartridge.
AMMUNITION CAPACITY:	9 pistol rounds, one shotgun
EFFECTIVE RANGE:	50m (164ft)
COMPLEXITY:	Fairly high
USERS:	Confederate Cavalry

The Le Mat revolver was an interesting idea that fulfilled a very real need. It was a failure mainly due to production values, although it is telling that there have been very few multi-calibre weapons in history.

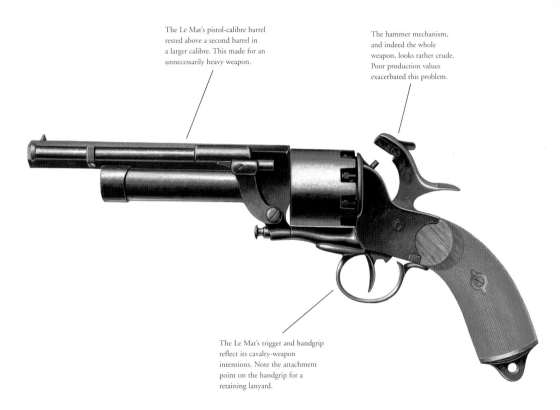

The Le Mat's pistol-calibre barrel rested above a second barrel in a larger calibre. This made for an unnecessarily heavy weapon.

The hammer mechanism, and indeed the whole weapon, looks rather crude. Poor production values exacerbated this problem.

The Le Mat's trigger and handgrip reflect its cavalry-weapon intentions. Note the attachment point on the handgrip for a retaining lanyard.

MODEL 1873 SPRINGFIELD CARBINE 1873

The standard US cavalry weapon of the late 1870s was the Model 1873 Springfield Carbine, a single-shot weapon with copper cartridges which tended to expand under the heat of rapid firing and jam the weapon. It was not especially bad, but it was out of date.

When General George Armstrong Custer led the 7th Cavalry to disaster at Little Big Horn in 1876, they came up against Native Americans armed with Spencer and Winchester repeating rifles, which could pour fire into the enemy ranks and – just as importantly – were less prone to become useless in combat. The results are well known.

SPECIFICATIONS

TYPE:	Longarm, cartridge
LENGTH:	1.1m (3ft 7in)
CALIBRE:	.45
AMMUNITION	
CAPACITY:	Single shot
EFFECTIVE	
RANGE:	100m (328ft)
COMPLEXITY:	Moderate
USERS:	US Cavalry

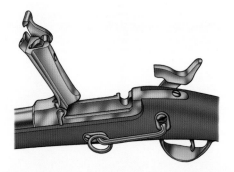

The Springfield 1873 carbine acquired the 'trapdoor' nickname for its loading mechanism. The weapon was reputed to be unreliable and prone to jamming among other reasons because the breech could fail to lock properly. Trooper confidence in these weapons was low.

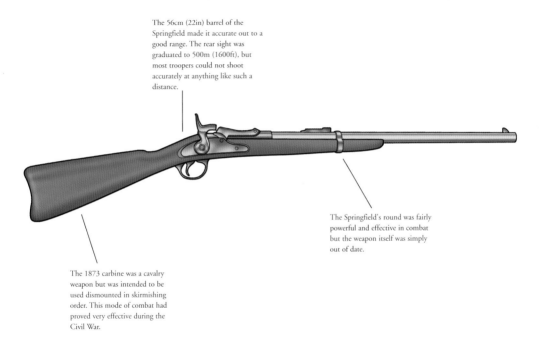

The 56cm (22in) barrel of the Springfield made it accurate out to a good range. The rear sight was graduated to 500m (1600ft), but most troopers could not shoot accurately at anything like such a distance.

The Springfield's round was fairly powerful and effective in combat but the weapon itself was simply out of date.

The 1873 carbine was a cavalry weapon but was intended to be used dismounted in skirmishing order. This mode of combat had proved very effective during the Civil War.

APACHE PISTOL *1880*

Taking the combination weapon concept to a very silly extreme was the 'Apache' pistol, named for the gangs of the late nineteenth century who carried these weapons. The Apache pistol consisted of a knuckle-duster, which forms the grip for a very small-calibre revolver. A short knife juts downward from the opposite end of the duster, creating a clumsy and rather flimsy contraption, which, in theory, allows the user to stab, slash or shoot their opponent whilst adding weight to a punch. In reality the Apache pistol was little more than a gimmick and was highly ineffective.

SPECIFICATIONS

TYPE:	Personal
LENGTH:	10–15cm (4–6in)
WEIGHT:	Less than 1kg (2lb)
RANGE:	Close combat or short
EASE OF USE:	Low
COMPOSITION:	Metal, flimsy but complex construction
USERS:	Street toughs

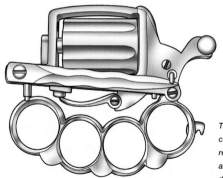

The Apache folded. In this configuration it makes a reasonable knuckle-duster – although no better than a normal duster.

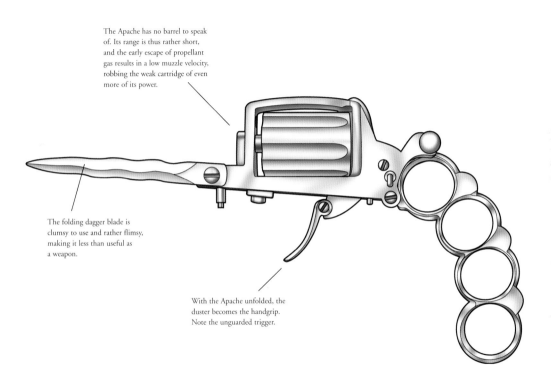

The Apache has no barrel to speak of. Its range is thus rather short, and the early escape of propellant gas results in a low muzzle velocity, robbing the weak cartridge of even more of its power.

The folding dagger blade is clumsy to use and rather flimsy, making it less than useful as a weapon.

With the Apache unfolded, the duster becomes the handgrip. Note the unguarded trigger.

MAUSER C/96 'BROOMHANDLE' 1896

Introduced in 1896, the Mauser 'Broomhandle' was in some ways an excellent weapon; however, it used a complex system of operation and was expensive to manufacture.

The downfall of this weapon was its capability to fire on fully automatic. Even the rather impractical 20-round magazine provided an inadequate ammunition supply, and the six- and ten-round versions were invariably empty before the user could begin to correct his aim. Handguns are not well suited to fully automatic fire because recoil drives the muzzle up rather rapidly, and full-auto fire with a C/96 was a good way to dispose of ammunition without being any real use in a firefight.

SPECIFICATIONS

TYPE:	Handgun, full-automatic capable
LENGTH:	31cm (12in)
CALIBRE:	7.63 or 9mm
AMMUNITION CAPACITY:	6, 10 or 20 rounds
EFFECTIVE RANGE:	60m (197ft)
COMPLEXITY:	Moderate
USERS:	Private, military

The classic lines of the Mauser. Basically a fine weapon, it was not well suited to fully automatic operation.

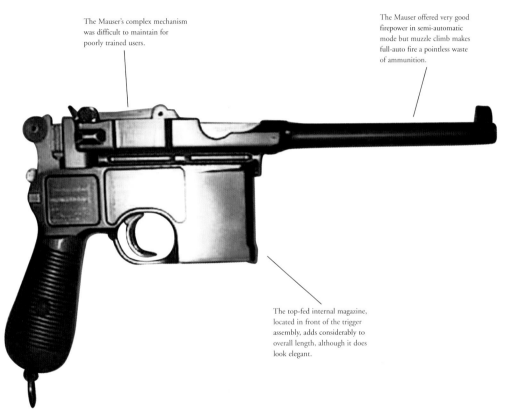

The Mauser's complex mechanism was difficult to maintain for poorly trained users.

The Mauser offered very good firepower in semi-automatic mode but muzzle climb makes full-auto fire a pointless waste of ammunition.

The top-fed internal magazine, located in front of the trigger assembly, adds considerably to overall length, although it does look elegant.

MARS PISTOL *1900*

At the beginning of the twentieth century, the self-loading pistol was attracting a lot of interest. Just a couple of decades before the classic Colt M1911 entered service, Hugh Gabbet-Fairfax patented the rather less effective Mars Self-loading Pistol.

The Mars was overcomplicated, relying on external cranks to load the next round using recoil energy. Its recoil was also very heavy, with spent cartridges being ejected straight back into the user's face. The combination of these factors and all the mechanical activity going on at the time made the Mars a very unpleasant weapon to fire. About 80 were made, after which the Mars quite rightly faded from the scene.

SPECIFICATIONS

TYPE:	Handgun
LENGTH:	25cm (10in)
CALIBRE:	Various including .45
AMMUNITION	
CAPACITY:	6 rounds
EFFECTIVE	
RANGE:	40m (131ft)
COMPLEXITY:	High
USERS:	Few, private

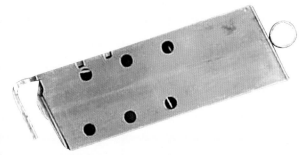

A Mars magazine. The weapon's six-round capacity offered no firepower advantage over a revolver other than the ability to change magazines quicker than manually loading a revolver. On top of that the Mars was overcomplex and unpleasant to shoot. There was simply no reason not to buy a revolver instead.

The Mars was considered as a military weapon but it was too difficult to maintain and its workings too prone to dirt to be successful.

The Mars could be chambered for various ammunition. Its .45 round was arguably the most powerful available at the time.

Firing the Mars resulted in a huge muzzle flash that was unpleasant for the user and bystanders, and caused an early version of 'magnum flinch'.

ROSS RIFLE 1903

Developed by Sir Charles Ross, the Ross Rifle seemed very promising at the outset. However, just because it performed nicely on the range did not mean it would stand up to combat conditions. Canadian troops in World War I found the Ross to be extremely intolerant of dirt and prone to jamming.

The very worst feature of the Ross was the fact that the bolt could be assembled with the bolt unattached to the receiver. The error would be discovered only when firing, when the bolt and rifle would part company to the detriment of weapon and soldier.

SPECIFICATIONS

TYPE:	Longarm
LENGTH:	1.3m (4ft)
CALIBRE:	.303
AMMUNITION CAPACITY:	5 rounds
EFFECTIVE RANGE:	1000m (3280ft)
COMPLEXITY:	Moderate
USERS:	Military (Canada)

While a good rifle on the range, the Ross was wholly unsuited to the harsh conditions of the trenches, and broke down quickly. In 1916 Douglas Haig ordered all Ross weapons discarded and replaced with Lee-Enfields.

When field-stripping a Ross, the user had to be very careful how it was put back together. This was not always easy under combat conditions.

Sir Charles Ross conceded that there were some 'small problems' with his rifle, but maintained that they could easily be fixed. He was proven wrong by conditions in the trenches.

33

GLISENTI MODEL M1910 PISTOL 1910

Derived from a 1907-vintage 7.56mm weapon, the M1910 was an updated 9mm version which in practice turned out to be a very poor weapon. Used with standard 9mm ammunition, the M1910 had an unfortunate tendency to explode due to weak construction. This left the user with a choice between using a specially developed underpowered cartridge or risking self-injury.

Some of the M1910's defects stemmed from an attempt by the designers to be clever. For instance, the entire left side of the weapon could be removed for cleaning, a convenient feature, but one which contributed to the pistol's overall uselessness as a weapon.

SPECIFICATIONS

TYPE:	Handgun
LENGTH:	21cm (8in)
CALIBRE:	9mm Glisenti
AMMUNITION CAPACITY:	7 rounds
EFFECTIVE RANGE:	20m (65ft 7in)
COMPLEXITY:	Moderate
USERS:	Military

The detachable left side of the weapon was meant as a convenience. It tended to detach itself when the weapon was fired, however, and this was not a well-liked feature.

The M1910 was chambered for ammunition its frame could not handle.

The M1910 clearly shows the dangers inherent in adapting a weapon for more powerful ammunition. Having increased the calibre to 9mm for more stopping power, the designers had to develop a weaker round that the gun could handle.

Holding only seven rounds, the M1910 had marginally more ammunition than a good .38 revolver and was less powerful.

HANDGUN BAYONETS *1915*

D uring World War I it was quickly discovered that rifles were too unwieldy for trench fighting. Knives, clubs, spades and handguns were much more suitable. The search for more effective trench-clearance weapons led to the invention of revolver-bayonets; a long spike or knife-type bayonet either on the barrel of a revolver or projecting downwards from the butt.

The addition of a blade simply unbalances a handgun, making it less effective in its intended role, while the blade itself is too unwieldy to make a useful weapon. Nevertheless, there are some modern weapons available with both a blade and a torch built in.

SPECIFICATIONS

TYPE:	Personal hand-to-hand
LENGTH:	15–25cm (6–9in)
WEIGHT:	Under 1kg (2lb)
RANGE:	Close combat
EASE OF USE:	High
COMPOSITION:	Steel
USERS:	Private users, sometimes in a military setting

A folding handgun bayonet. The user would be better off with either a knife or a handgun, rather than something that tried to be both and failed.

A handgun's primary purpose is to shoot bullets. Anything that detracts from this function is a mistake as it makes the weapon less, not more, useful to the wielder.

An early handgun/blade experiment. Thrusting with a pistol-mounted blade is a clumsy business, and this awkwardness could cost the user his life in a trench melee.

CHAUCHAT MACHINE GUN 1915

B uilt badly and cheaply to a very poor design, the Chauchat was hated by the American, Belgian, French and Greek troops who had to use it. Its long-recoil action was rather violent, making the weapon hard to control. The rimmed 8mm Lebel round was not very suitable to machine-gun use and added to the inbuilt tendency of the Chauchat to jam even when firing at a rather modest 250rpm. Many examples of the Chauchat were poorly machined and badly put together, as if the production crews knew that this was a weapon on which it was not worth wasting any effort.

SPECIFICATIONS

TYPE:	Support weapon
LENGTH:	1.2m (4ft)
CALIBRE:	8x50mm Lebel
EFFECTIVE RANGE:	1000m (3280ft)
COMPLEXITY:	Moderate
USERS:	Military (France, Belgium, Greece and USA)

A French machine-gunner gamely does his best with the appalling Chauchat. Relying on such weapons to stop an enemy assault or suppress troops could lead to life-threatening disappointment.

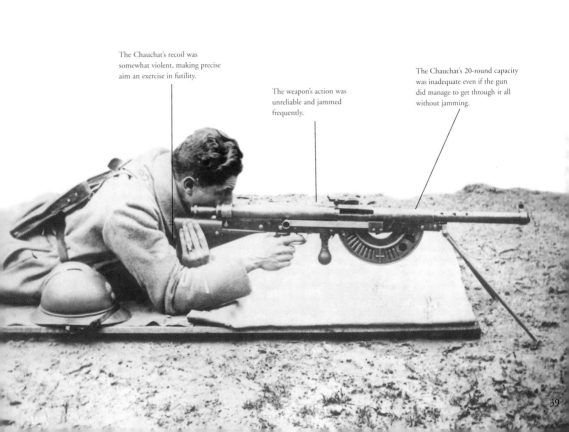

The Chauchat's recoil was somewhat violent, making precise aim an exercise in futility.

The weapon's action was unreliable and jammed frequently.

The Chauchat's 20-round capacity was inadequate even if the gun did manage to get through it all without jamming.

PISTOLE MITRAGLIATRICE VILAR-PEROSA M15 1915

The Vilar-Perosa was a top-fed double-barrelled weapon originally intended for use in the support role by mountain troops, but eventually taken into general use by Italian forces through both World Wars.

The Vilar-Perosa could empty both 25-round magazines very quickly as it fired at 1200rpm, making sustained fire support less than effective. This impressive though brief firepower was exploited by fitting the weapon with straps to allow it to be fired from the hip on the move. The result was a weapon capable of spraying a very large amount of bullets around the countryside in a short period, and more or less at random.

SPECIFICATIONS

TYPE:	Support weapon
LENGTH:	53cm (21in)
CALIBRE:	9mm Glisenti
AMMUNITION CAPACITY:	2 x 25 rounds
EFFECTIVE RANGE:	120m (395ft)
COMPLEXITY:	Fairly high
USERS:	Military (Italy)

The Vilar-Perosa M15 was not such a bad weapon, but it was before its time and was not very effective in its intended role. Its main flaw was low ammunition capacity coupled with high rate of fire.

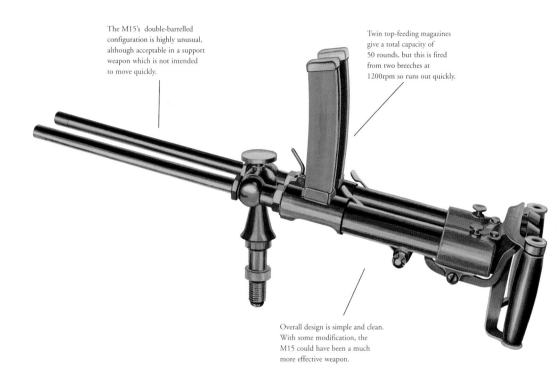

The M15's double-barrelled configuration is highly unusual, although acceptable in a support weapon which is not intended to move quickly.

Twin top-feeding magazines give a total capacity of 50 rounds, but this is fired from two breeches at 1200rpm so runs out quickly.

Overall design is simple and clean. With some modification, the M15 could have been a much more effective weapon.

NAMBU 94 1934

Vehicle crews and aircraft pilots fielded another version of the appalling Nambu 14, known as the 94. It was no better and used the same weak 8mm cartridge. It also had a tendency to go off when knocked against something hard, which can be a problem when boarding a vehicle! The only virtues of the Type 94 were smaller size and slightly better reliability than the Nambu 14, which is not saying much. This was not due to improved design, but rather to the fact that it suffered from less exposure to the elements when carried by a vehicle or aircraft crewmember.

The Imperial Japanese armed forces did not consider pistols to be serious combat weapons. This is probably just as well, given the performance of the weapons they issued. This vehicle crewman's sword is probably more useful as a battlefield weapon than his handgun.

SPECIFICATIONS

TYPE:	Handgun
LENGTH:	23cm (9in)
CALIBRE:	8mm Nambu
AMMUNITION CAPACITY:	8 rounds
EFFECTIVE RANGE:	30m (98ft)
COMPLEXITY:	Moderate
USERS:	Military

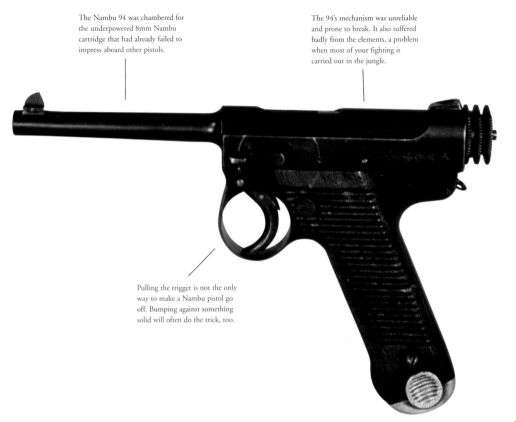

The Nambu 94 was chambered for the underpowered 8mm Nambu cartridge that had already failed to impress aboard other pistols.

The 94's mechanism was unreliable and prone to break. It also suffered badly from the elements, a problem when most of your fighting is carried out in the jungle.

Pulling the trigger is not the only way to make a Nambu pistol go off. Bumping against something solid will often do the trick, too.

ANTITANK RIFLES *1937*

SPECIFICATIONS

TYPE:	Infantry antimateriel weapon
LENGTH:	1.6m (5ft)
CALIBRE:	7.92 to 14mm
AMMUNITION CAPACITY:	5 rounds typically
EFFECTIVE RANGE:	100m (328ft)
COMPLEXITY:	Moderate
USERS:	Military (various nations)

Various attempts have been made to provide infantry with a useful antitank weapon that could move with them. One solution to the problem was the *Panzerbüchse*, or antitank rifle.

Many weapons were fielded by different powers. Firing an armour-piercing round in calibres from 7.92 to 14mm, antitank rifles were capable of penetrating the armour of early tanks but were quickly outmoded by better armour. Another drawback was that a tank is a large object and a bullet makes a small hole. It was entirely possible to achieve penetration but not hit anything important, and since these were bolt-action weapons firing a single round, firepower was not great.

A German soldier selects from a large number of antitank rifles. While better than nothing, these weapons were only effective against early or light armoured vehicles, and were mainly kept in service for lack of anything better.

Large, heavy and difficult to move around with, antitank rifles could be used only by positioned troops.

The weapon's long barrel imparted an impressive muzzle velocity and helped to soak up recoil to tolerable levels.

Versions fielded by various nations ranged considerably in calibre. Many used heavy machine-gun rounds or special armour-piercing versions of them.

CZ38 PISTOL 1938

The CZ38 seems to be an attempt to make up for the many very good guns to come out of the former country of Czechoslovakia, and this is the only thing at which it succeeds.

Chambered for the weak 9mm short (.380) round, the CZ38 carries eight rounds in its magazine, and ensures that none of them will go near the target with an extremely heavy trigger pull. This is due to the self-cocking action the weapon uses – it cannot be cocked and fired single-action for improved accuracy. All this mediocrity was presented in a singularly unattractive package that weighed more than the contemporary Browning and carried five rounds fewer.

SPECIFICATIONS

TYPE:	Handgun
LENGTH:	21cm (8in)
CALIBRE:	9mm short
AMMUNITION	
CAPACITY:	8 rounds
EFFECTIVE	
RANGE:	30m (98ft)
COMPLEXITY:	Moderate
USERS:	Military

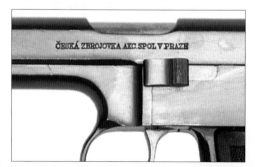

The CZ38 was underpowered, inaccurate and generally a pig to shoot with. Its clumsy design did nothing for its looks or reputation.

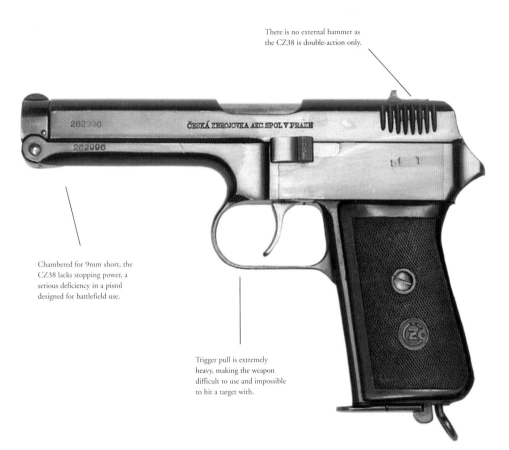

There is no external hammer as the CZ38 is double-action only.

Chambered for 9mm short, the CZ38 lacks stopping power, a serious deficiency in a pistol designed for battlefield use.

Trigger pull is extremely heavy, making the weapon difficult to use and impossible to hit a target with.

ČESKÁ ZBROJOVKA AKC SPOL V PRAZE

262996

262996

One way to overcome the inadequacy of antitank rifles was to use special ammunition. The Mauser *Panzerbüchse* 39 was originally equipped with a clever round consisting of a steel penetrator and a capsule of tear gas. The idea was that, even if the penetrator did not disable the tank, the gas would make it untenable and force the crew to abandon their vehicle.

In practice, what usually happened was that the gas capsule broke off and was left outside the armour, creating an additional hazard for infantry who might be trying to disable the tank through close assault.

SPECIFICATIONS

TYPE:	Ammunition
ROLE:	Antitank, special capability
CALIBRE:	7.92mm
COMPOSITION:	Steel penetrator plus tear-gas capsule
PENETRATION:	30mm (1in) of armour at 100m (328ft)
COMPLEXITY:	Fairly high
USERS:	Military (Germany)

The extreme outer limit of infantry weapons; a very large antitank rifle on a wheeled carriage. Unsure if it is an infantry or an artillery weapon, the anti-tank rifle is ineffective in either role.

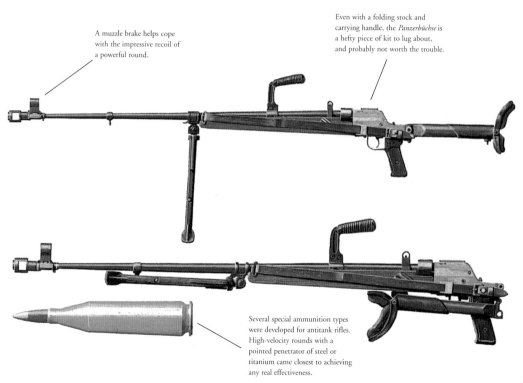

A muzzle brake helps cope with the impressive recoil of a powerful round.

Even with a folding stock and carrying handle, the *Panzerbüchse* is a hefty piece of kit to lug about, and probably not worth the trouble.

Several special ammunition types were developed for antitank rifles. High-velocity rounds with a pointed penetrator of steel or titanium came closest to achieving any real effectiveness.

NORTHOVER PROJECTOR *1940*

The Northover Projector was intended to give the Home Guard a measure of support and even antitank capability. It consisted of what looked suspiciously like a length of drain pipe on a tripod with a crude feed mechanism. It fired a range of grenades including a white phosphorous projectile, using a black powder charge initiated by a percussion cap. Variants included a version fed by a revolving magazine.

Neither the projector nor its variants was much good, having a maximum range of just 200m (656ft), but it is safe to say that they would have been crewed with great valour and determination had the invasion come.

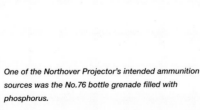

One of the Northover Projector's intended ammunition sources was the No.76 bottle grenade filled with phosphorus.

SPECIFICATIONS

TYPE:	Unguided antitank weapon
WEIGHT:	33.6kg (74lb) with mountings
PAYLOAD:	63.5mm (2½in) antitank or incendiary grenade
AMMUNITION CAPACITY:	Single shot
EFFECTIVE RANGE:	100m (328ft)
COMPLEXITY:	Low
USERS:	Home Guard (UK)

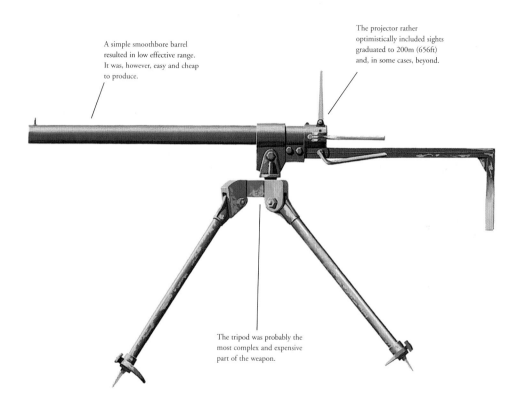

A simple smoothbore barrel resulted in low effective range. It was, however, easy and cheap to produce.

The projector rather optimistically included sights graduated to 200m (656ft) and, in some cases, beyond.

The tripod was probably the most complex and expensive part of the weapon.

INVASION PIKES *1940*

With its army in tatters and faced with imminent invasion, Britain in 1940 was a hive of improvisation and invention. All manner of weaponry was pressed into service to arm the Home Guard. One particularly strange idea was to try to oppose the panzers with 'invasion pikes'. These consisted of a bayonet welded to a short haft. It is open to debate exactly what the users were supposed to do with these weapons, and it is perhaps unsurprising that the few pikes that were put together were dumped in a warehouse and forgotten about.

SPECIFICATIONS

TYPE:	Personal hand to hand
LENGTH:	1–1.5m (3–5ft)
WEIGHT:	1–2kg (2–4¼lb)
RANGE:	Hand to hand
EASE OF USE:	High
COMPOSITION:	Metal, crude welding
USERS:	Home Guard (UK)

Much fun has been poked at the Home Guard over the years, but the truth is that its personnel were prepared to fight with tooth, nail and, if necessary, pike against an invasion of Britain.

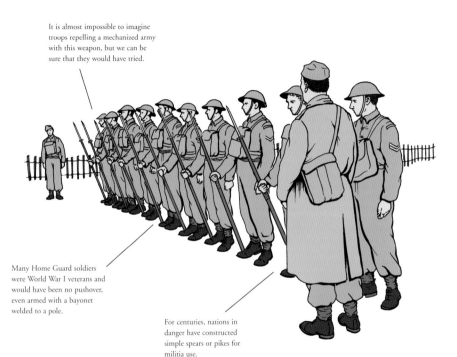

It is almost impossible to imagine troops repelling a mechanized army with this weapon, but we can be sure that they would have tried.

Many Home Guard soldiers were World War I veterans and would have been no pushover, even armed with a bayonet welded to a pole.

For centuries, nations in danger have constructed simple spears or pikes for militia use.

STEN GUN MK II *1940*

The Mark II is the definitive Sten submachine gun. Resembling a roughly machined collection of scrap metal, it could be quite exciting to be around, as it tended to go off when knocked. Magazines were also of very inferior quality, which further reduced reliability. Old soldiers report a rather poor performance at range – including tales of bullets bouncing off a thick greatcoat!

The Sten was a huge success for the simple reason that it was so crude. At a time when Britain faced invasion and vast numbers of weapons were needed, the Sten was quick and easy to put together, and it was a lot better than nothing.

SPECIFICATIONS

TYPE:	Submachine gun
LENGTH:	76cm (30in)
CALIBRE:	9mm Parabellum
AMMUNITION CAPACITY:	32 rounds
EFFECTIVE RANGE:	70m (230ft)
COMPLEXITY:	Low
USERS	Military, Home Guard, resistance fighters

Better than a pike, the Sten gun became one of the classic weapons of World War II. Germany put a very similar weapon into production when the tide of war turned against her.

The Sten's action left a lot to be desired. Ammunition feed remained a problem through several versions of the weapon.

The steel stock and buttplate were not comfortable to use but they got the job done.

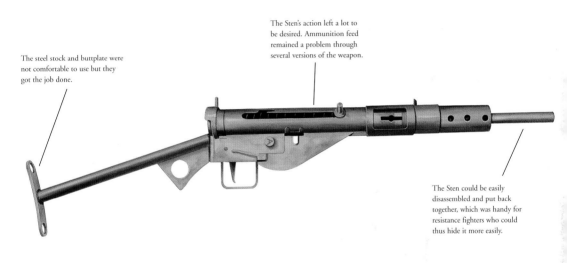

The Sten could be easily disassembled and put back together, which was handy for resistance fighters who could thus hide it more easily.

FURRER MP41/44 1941

With World War II in full swing, the Swiss Army of 1940 needed a submachine gun in a hurry, and, like all rush jobs, the project resulted in a less-than-satisfactory weapon.

With its large-capacity 40-round box magazine, the Furrer was clumsy and awkward to use, which reduced efficiency. However, the main flaw with the MP41 was its vast overcomplexity. Its internal workings attempted to adapt the Maxim toggle-lock to a small lightweight weapon, without undue success. The MP41 was thus slow and expensive to manufacture and difficult to use effectively. It did not enter service until 1944 due to manufacturing issues, by which time it was unnecessary anyway.

SPECIFICATIONS

TYPE:	Submachine gun
LENGTH:	77.5cm (30½in)
CALIBRE:	9mm Parabellum
AMMUNITION	
CAPACITY:	40 rounds
EFFECTIVE	
RANGE:	70m (230ft)
COMPLEXITY:	High
USERS:	Few; the projected clients bought elsewhere

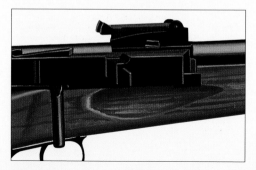

The Furrer MP41/44 was a horribly overcomplicated weapon. Its internal workings were based on the Mauser action, which may have been excellent for rifles, but was less than ideal for a submachine gun.

The Furrer bears a superficial resemblance to other submachine guns of the time such as the Lanchester and PPSh41. Internally it is quite different, being more complex. It was also more difficult to build and use than these more successful weapons.

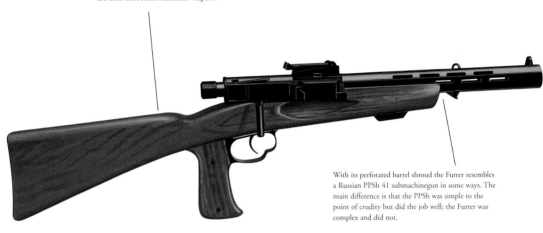

With its perforated barrel shroud the Furrer resembles a Russian PPSh 41 submachinegun in some ways. The main difference is that the PPSh was simple to the point of crudity but did the job well; the Furrer was complex and did not.

BAZOOKA 1942

Somewhat better than the PIAT, the Bazooka looks a lot more businesslike, although its 60mm (2½in) shaped-charge warhead was not very much more effective. The bazooka was lighter than a PIAT and simpler to produce in numbers, giving a marginal anti-armour capability to infantry.

One major drawback of the bazooka (in addition to its tendency to

bounce off tanks without harming them) was the huge backblast that pinpointed the firer's position to anyone who might mean him harm. The best thing about the bazooka was that it formed the basis for better weapons that came along later.

The Bazooka broke down into parts for carrying, making it possible for infantry forces to have an integral if marginal antitank capability. It was also simple and cheap to produce, which partially made up for the fact that it was not very good.

SPECIFICATIONS

TYPE:	Unguided antitank weapon
WEIGHT:	1.4m (4ft 6in)
PAYLOAD:	1.6kg (3½lb) shaped-charge high explosive
AMMUNITION CAPACITY:	Single Shot Rocket Launcher
EFFECTIVE RANGE:	150m (492ft)
COMPLEXITY:	Low
USERS:	Military (USA)

The Bazooka's 60mm warhead was marginally useful against tanks and could be fired at other targets such as bunkers and machine-gun nests.

The backblast from a rocket leaving the muzzle was directed at the firer's face, so most versions of the bazooka incorporated some kind of shield.

The weapon tended to throw up a lot of dust and debris when fired. This pinpointed the user's position and attracted enemy fire.

59

TYPE 100 SUBMACHINE GUN 1942

By the time the Type 100 was put into production in 1942, it was already obsolete, and it would never have been any good, even had it entered service two decades earlier. A clumsy side-loading design using a 30-round magazine, the Type 100 had a rate of fire of only 400rpm – extremely slow by SMG standards. Its potential performance was further degraded by the highly unimpressive 8mm Nambu handgun round and to cap it all the Type 100 tended to jam. Production ceased in 1943, but was restarted a year later with the very slightly less bad Type 100/44 model.

SPECIFICATIONS

TYPE:	Submachine gun
LENGTH:	89cm (35in)
CALIBRE:	8mm Nambu
AMMUNITION	
CAPACITY:	30 rounds
EFFECTIVE	
RANGE:	70m (230ft)
COMPLEXITY:	Moderate
USERS:	Military (Japan)

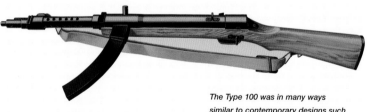

*The Type 100 was in many ways
similar to contemporary designs such
as the excellent Lanchester; however,
the only thing it had in common with
the Lanchester was a side-loading
magazine and wooden furniture.*

The Type 100 action was very unreliable and prone to jamming.

The designers chose to use the Nambu 8mm pistol round, presumably for availability reasons. Whatever other faults the Type 100 had, its ammunition alone condemned it to mediocrity.

A clumsy and slow-firing weapon, the Type 100 was obsolescent when it went into service. World War I saw the first really modern submachine guns appear; the Type 100 belongs to an earlier age.

BROWNING M1919A6 *1943*

The Browning M1919 is one of history's very best and longest-lived firearms. An air-cooled medium machine gun firing a powerful .30 cartridge, the weapon served for many years, including the whole of World War II.

Almost inevitably, variants appeared. Some were excellent, but the 1943-vintage 'A6' was not one of them. Basically it was an M1919 fitted with a butt for shoulder firing and a bipod. The concept was reasonable enough, but the result was a clumsy and heavy weapon weighing 14kg (31lb) unloaded. The M1919 was designed to be used from a mount and it did not convert well to an infantry role.

SPECIFICATIONS

TYPE:	Support weapon
LENGTH:	1.2m (4ft)
CALIBRE:	.30 Browning
AMMUNITION CAPACITY:	250-round belt
EFFECTIVE RANGE:	2000m (6560ft)
COMPLEXITY:	Moderate
USERS:	Military (USA)

Pushed into a role it was not well suited for, the M1919A6 underperformed in the infantry squad support role and was not a success.

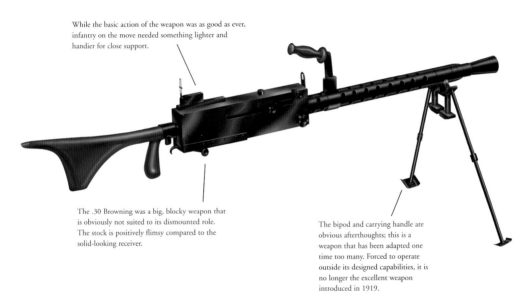

While the basic action of the weapon was as good as ever, infantry on the move needed something lighter and handier for close support.

The .30 Browning was a big, blocky weapon that is obviously not suited to its dismounted role. The stock is positively flimsy compared to the solid-looking receiver.

The bipod and carrying handle are obvious afterthoughts; this is a weapon that has been adapted one time too many. Forced to operate outside its designed capabilities, it is no longer the excellent weapon introduced in 1919.

PIAT 1943

The PIAT (Projectile, Infantry, Antitank) was a British attempt to come up with a decent infantry antitank weapon. It was not a great success, although it was better than nothing. It consisted of a bulky tube launcher that fired a rocket-propelled shaped-charge grenade.

The PIAT was only marginally effective against armour and then only from the sides or rear. It was useful at all at only quite short ranges, in return for all of which it was heavy and clumsy. Troops considered it inferior to the bazooka and would readily fling it away if they could replace it with a couple of German *Panzerfausts*.

SPECIFICATIONS

TYPE:	Unguided antitank weapon
WEIGHT:	99cm (39in)
PAYLOAD:	1.35kg (3lb) shaped-charge high explosive
AMMUNITION CAPACITY:	Single shot
EFFECTIVE RANGE:	100m (328ft)
COMPLEXITY:	Low
USERS:	Military (UK)

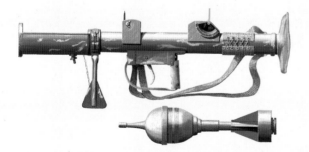

The PIAT, or 'drainpipe', and its projectile. Weapons of this type are sometimes referred to as spigot mortars, but whatever label is applied the PIAT is simply not very good.

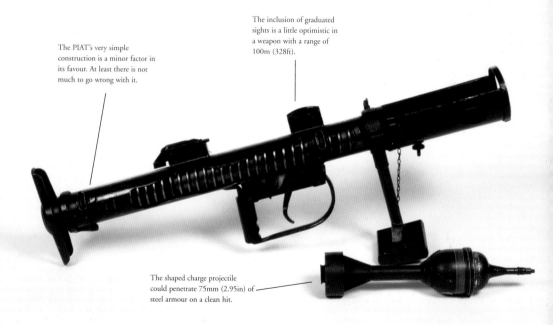

The PIAT's very simple construction is a minor factor in its favour. At least there is not much to go wrong with it.

The inclusion of graduated sights is a little optimistic in a weapon with a range of 100m (328ft).

The shaped charge projectile could penetrate 75mm (2.95in) of steel armour on a clean hit.

KRUMMLAUF *1945*

The Krummlauf was an attempt to provide troops with the capability to shoot round corners. It had a barrel curved between 30 and 45 degrees, and mounted a periscope sight to allow it to be poked round a corner without the user being exposed to return fire. Although it seems to be an infantryman's dream the Krummlauf was actually intended to allow vehicle crews to dispose of nearby infantry without leaving their armoured protection. The Krummlauf cost a lot to develop and was sufficiently unsuccessful that the experiment has not been repeated.

SPECIFICATIONS

TYPE:	Longarm
LENGTH:	1.2m (4ft)
CALIBRE:	7.62mm
AMMUNITION CAPACITY:	30 rounds
EFFECTIVE RANGE:	2000m (6561ft)
COMPLEXITY:	Fairly high
USERS:	Military (Germany)

Many variants of the Krummlauf were constructed. This one is particularly radical and is capable of shooting around a 90-degree corner. Other versions were built with 45-degree and 30-degree barrels, as well as variants with a fairly small curve to the barrel.

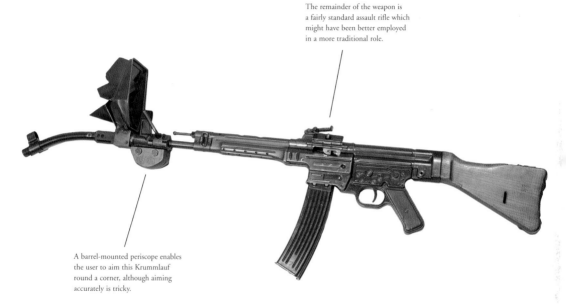

The remainder of the weapon is a fairly standard assault rifle which might have been better employed in a more traditional role.

A barrel-mounted periscope enables the user to aim this Krummlauf round a corner, although aiming accurately is tricky.

AK47 1947

Firing a short 7.62x39mm cartridge on semi- or full-automatic modes, the AK47 was one of the first assault rifles in the world, and in many ways it is not a good weapon. Its recoil is unpleasant; it is awkward to use with the cocking handle on the wrong side and a counterintuitive fire selector switch. It is also not very accurate.

And yet due to the incredibly robust and almost totally idiotproof design, the 'AK' has gone on to be a world-beater. It is particularly popular with conscript armies and militia.

SPECIFICATIONS

TYPE:	Longarm
LENGTH:	88cm (35in)
CALIBRE:	7.62x39mm
AMMUNITION CAPACITY:	30 rounds
EFFECTIVE RANGE:	300m (985ft)
COMPLEXITY:	Low
USERS:	Various; the AK series is in use worldwide

Showing the longevity of the design, this weapon is an AK-74, a derivative of the classic AK47 and developed more than 25 years later to the same basic design. The 'Kalashnikov' has become one of the world's great weapons, even though in many ways it is not a particularly good one.

The basic Kalashnikov action is simple and unbelievably robust, functioning reliably in the most difficult of environments.

The AK47 is capable of fairly accurate fire out to about 400m (1312ft), although it is sighted to greater ranges.

Simple but tough construction allows the 'AK' to thrive on maltreatment and neglect that would break most other weapons.

MAKAROV PISTOL 1957

The 1950s-vintage Makarov is typical of Russian handguns, which have never been considered to be serious combat weapons. Although small and easy to carry, and fairly well made from good materials, the Makarov is hampered by two main problems.

Firstly, the 9x18mm round used by the Makarov is weak and offers little stopping power, and there are not even very many of them as the Makarov has only an eight-round magazine. Secondly, while accurate shooting is difficult with any handgun, the Makarov's universally bad trigger action makes any sort of marksmanship an exercise in blind luck.

SPECIFICATIONS

TYPE:	Handgun
LENGTH:	16cm (6in)
CALIBRE:	9x18mm Soviet
AMMUNITION CAPACITY:	8 rounds
EFFECTIVE RANGE:	40m (131ft)
COMPLEXITY:	Moderate
USERS:	Military

Soviet and Russian forces have never considered pistols to be much more than status symbols or emergency weapons. The Makarov is reliable and makes a decent-enough threat, but is not a weapon on which to trust your life.

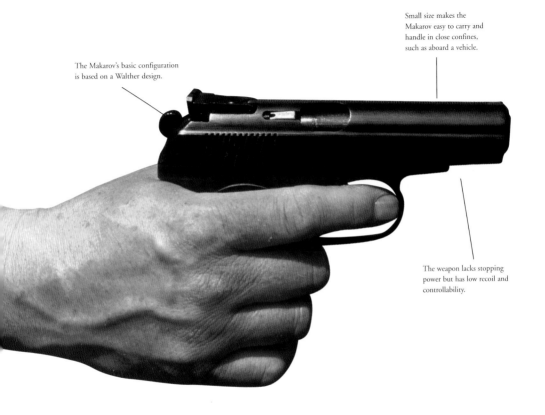

The Makarov's basic configuration is based on a Walther design.

Small size makes the Makarov easy to carry and handle in close confines, such as aboard a vehicle.

The weapon lacks stopping power but has low recoil and controllability.

M16 EARLY VERSIONS 1960

The M16 assault rifle suffered from some serious flaws when it was first introduced. M16s failed quickly in the filthy Vietnam jungle. As the weapon was designed not to need cleaning, no cleaning kits were available. Another problem with early M16s was the tendency of the plastic butt and furniture to become brittle in very cold conditions. This could lead to a broken rifle, as soldiers are not renowned for their gentleness when moving around or taking cover under fire. Later versions corrected these problems, but the early M16 was not a good weapon at all.

SPECIFICATIONS

TYPE:	Longarm
LENGTH:	1m (3ft)
CALIBRE:	5.56x45mm
AMMUNITION CAPACITY:	30 rounds
EFFECTIVE RANGE:	1000m (3280ft)
COMPLEXITY:	Moderate
USERS:	Military, worldwide

US troops deployed to Vietnam had high hopes for these new wonder rifles that did not need cleaning. The M16 fell far short of expectations, although it did mature into a decent weapon.

The M16 is still intolerant of dirt and grit in its mechanism, and needs to be looked after carefully. Troops in Iraq discovered this to their cost.

The M16 is sighted out to long ranges and is very accurate; few soldiers can effectively use the weapon's long accurate range.

The distinctive plastic barrel shroud has become a trademark of the M16 and its offspring, which include the Colt Commando.

M60 MACHINE GUN 1960

US troops refer to the M60 General Purpose Machine Gun as the 'pig', and not without reason. Changing barrels on the early M60 models was extremely difficult. An asbestos glove was required to handle the barrels and without it, changing was impossible. The weapon itself is not tolerant of abuse or dirt, and has a tendency to jam if given any excuse. Since its design in the late 1950s the M60 has steadily improved. Many believe the weapon has now achieved a high standard of mediocrity, but was such a poor design to begin with that further improvements are unlikely.

SPECIFICATIONS

TYPE:	Support weapon
LENGTH:	1.1m (3ft 7in)
CALIBRE:	7.62x51mm
AMMUNITION	
CAPACITY:	Belt-fed
EFFECTIVE	
RANGE:	3000m (9,842ft)
COMPLEXITY:	Moderate
USERS:	Military (USA)

The M60 has been a standard support weapon of US forces since the 1960s. Many versions have been created, all of which tried to improve on a fairly poor basic design.

The M60's barrel is lined with Stellite, allowing it to be fired even when white-hot. This does not do the barrel much good, however, and regular changes are necessary for long life.

The M60's basic action is now more reliable than earlier versions, but it retains some of the original's faults, including intolerance of environmental conditions.

Although 5.56mm support weapons are becoming more and more popular, the hard-hitting 7.62mm ammunition used by the M60 is well respected. This may keep the M60 in service for many years yet.

SAMOPAL 62 SKORPION *1961*

Firing a fairly weak 7.65 (.32) round from a seven-round magazine, the Skorpion is a fully-automatic handgun-sized weapon. Muzzle climb under full-auto fire is impressive, and its general randomness is enhanced by its clever rate-of-fire limiter. This consists of a weight bouncing up and down on a spring in the grip, which does nothing to enhance accuracy.

The result is a weapon with a shorter accurate range than a handgun and containing less ammunition than most, and which is hard to control. At extreme close quarters it is a deadly weapon and is prized by terrorists.

SPECIFICATIONS

TYPE:	Assault pistol
LENGTH:	27cm (10in)
CALIBRE:	32 ACP (7.65mm)
AMMUNITION CAPACITY:	7 rounds
EFFECTIVE RANGE:	20m (65ft 7in)
COMPLEXITY:	Moderate
USERS:	Military (vehicle crews) and paramilitary/terrorists

The folded stock is a trademark of the Skorpion. The weapon's main advantage is its small size, so few users bother to extend the stock. Doing this does little to improve accuracy anyway.

The Skorpion is only slightly longer than the average handgun and offers full-auto capability. This may or may not be seen as an advantage.

The standard magazine holds seven rounds, but larger-capacity magazines are available. These, however, make the Skorpion a lot more bulky.

Rate of fire is kept down to sane levels by an ingenious device in the butt. It consists of a weight on a spring, which is not conducive to controllability.

77

GYROJET PISTOL 1965

The Gyrojet was developed in the 1960s as an alternative to conventional firearms. Rather than firing an inert projectile using the explosion of gases in the firing chamber, the Gyrojet used rocket propulsion to accelerate its ammunition.

In addition to a very small magazine capacity of just six rounds, the Gyrojet also suffers from a very poor performance at short range and a general lack of accuracy. Some examples were taken to Vietnam, where they failed to achieve anything very useful. Even the possibility of launching an explosive-tipped version of the standard rocket ammunition did not attract interest, and the Gyrojet faded into the background as a curiosity.

SPECIFICATIONS

TYPE:	Handgun
LENGTH:	30cm (12in)
CALIBRE:	13x50mm rocket
AMMUNITION CAPACITY:	6 rounds
EFFECTIVE RANGE:	50m (165ft)
COMPLEXITY:	High
USERS:	Private, some military

The Gyrojet is an ingenious device which failed to cope when it met reality head-on. Although it did demonstrate an interesting concept, the Gyrojet never developed into a practical weapon.

78

The gyrojet has no ejection port, as the entire round is launched from the barrel. This reduces the number of moving parts and susceptibility to dirt.

Rather than a standard bullet, the Gyrojet launches a self-propelled rocket.

Even 40 years on, the Gyrojet looks like something from science fiction. Thought by some to be the future of firearms, it turned out to be a blind alley instead.

M73/M219 MACHINE GUN 1967

esigned in the 1950s and introduced in 1967, the M73 was conceived as a lightweight weapon for co-axial and pintle-mounted vehicle use. Firing a standard NATO 7.62 round, the weapon should have been straightforward enough. It malfunctioned so often, however, that some users compared it unfavourably to the dreadful Chauchat.

An 'improved' E1 model and later the redesignated M219 were fielded, but represented little real improvement. Israeli forces hated these weapons so much as a result of experiences in the 1973 Yom Kippur War that an immediate replacement was sought.

SPECIFICATIONS

TYPE:	Support weapon
LENGTH:	89cm (35in)
CALIBRE:	7.62x51mm
AMMUNITION	
CAPACITY:	Belt-fed
EFFECTIVE	
RANGE:	900m (2950ft)
COMPLEXITY:	Moderate
USERS:	US (vehicle mount)

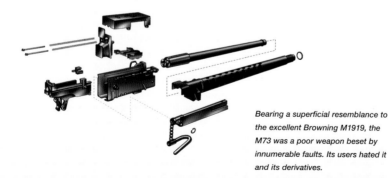

Bearing a superficial resemblance to the excellent Browning M1919, the M73 was a poor weapon beset by innumerable faults. Its users hated it and its derivatives.

The M73 is usually fed from the left, but can be easily reconfigured for right-hand feed.

The M73 is recoil operated and air cooled, a well-proven mode of operation. Despite this, the M73 demonstrates that it is still possible to get it wrong.

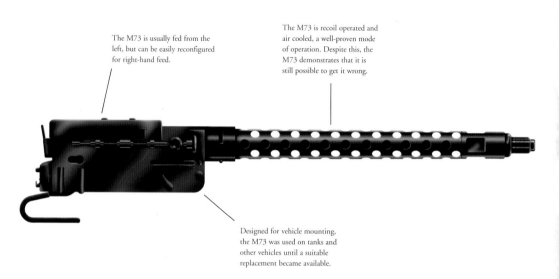

Designed for vehicle mounting, the M73 was used on tanks and other vehicles until a suitable replacement became available.

TASERS 1969

Tasers fire a pair of small darts which, upon lodging in the target, allow a high-voltage electric current to be delivered. This will render the victim incapable of action without killing him. Tasers are easily defeated by heavy clothing, however, even assuming the user can shoot accurately enough to hit the target with both darts, and reloading takes too long to be viable in combat. It is perhaps telling that when police use tasers on a suspect, several other officers stand by to use more robust methods if the taser fails to have the desired effect.

SPECIFICATIONS

TYPE: Non-lethal ranged
LENGTH: 15–30cm (6–12in)
WEIGHT: 0.5kg (1lb)
RANGE: 10m (32ft)
EASE OF USE: Moderate
COMPOSITION: Plastics, electronic
               components, advanced
               construction
USERS: Law enforcement, security

A futuristic weapon, here seen fitted with a laser sighting aid, the taser has many law enforcement uses, but is not very suitable for self-defence as it simply cannot be relied upon to stop the 'bad guy'.

Twin darts are housed in the front of the weapon, with the power supply in the grip. Note the handgun-style safety catch at the rear.

The taser's plastic construction gives it a clean, elegant – some would say toylike – appearance.

SA80 EARLY VERSIONS *1985*

A 'bullpup' design ideal for urban and vehicle-borne combat, the SA80 should have been an excellent weapon. Unfortunately, it was not. Early users had to contend with a cocking handle that sometimes detached itself from the bolt, leaving the weapon useless, and a magazine release that could be activated by simply carrying the weapon in the normal position.

On top of all of this, some early SA80s are reported as becoming brittle in cold conditions and literally breaking on contact with something hard. The weapon is also not very tolerant of dirt, which can be a drawback.

SPECIFICATIONS

TYPE:	Longarm
LENGTH:	78.5cm (31in)
CALIBRE:	5.56x45mm
AMMUNITION	
CAPACITY:	30 rounds
EFFECTIVE	
RANGE:	400m (1312ft)
COMPLEXITY:	Moderate
USERS:	Military (UK)

The SA80 is, in theory, ideal for urban combat. It is short and handy, yet offers both devastating close-range firepower and long-range accuracy. As a weapon, however, it suffers from some drawbacks, including reliability problems.

The SA80's smaller size and lighter weight compared to the previous British Army rifle, the FN FAL, are welcome features for heavily loaded troops.

Blank firing adapters allow realistic training without using full-power cartridges.

Easy to carry yet telescoping out to a useful length at need, the action of deploying this weapon can be intimidating to the intended victim, and, in principle, it seems to be a useful design.

However, the flicking action needed to deploy the weapon can result in accidental injury to comrades if due care is not taken, and sometimes a well-used baton will fail to deploy or immediately collapse back on itself. Coupled with the fact that these weapons are not nearly as effective as they look unless the weighted head strikes a vulnerable spot, this makes the extendable baton a less-than-ideal weapon.

SPECIFICATIONS

TYPE:	Personal hand to hand
LENGTH:	40–65cm (15–25in)
WEIGHT:	0.5kg–0.75kg (1–1½lb)
RANGE:	Close combat
EASE OF USE:	Moderate
COMPOSITION:	Steel, complex
USERS:	Police, security

Training with an extendable baton. In theory, an extendable baton offers all the advantages of a more traditional weapon in an easy-to-carry package.

When in carrying mode, a telescopic baton is a small package.

Once extended, the baton becomes a useful weapon. The carry tube becomes the weapon's handle.

Various types are available; all are variations on the same basic theme.

87

VEHICLES AND ARTILLERY

Combat vehicles must above all be mobile. They need a reliable source of power and the means to deliver this power to the ground, driving the vehicle. They also need to be able to cope with obstacles and rough ground, and to protect the crew from a suitable level of threat. If they can do these things they may be a success as a vehicle, though to be a combat vehicle they need more. A successful combat vehicle also needs a weapon system that can hit its target and damage or destroy it.

Similar comments apply to artillery weapons. For the payload to be effective, it is necessary for it to be delivered accurately to the target. Range is important, and a big warhead makes up for inaccuracy to some degree. Overall, though, to be successful, an artillery weapon must put a useful payload somewhere near the enemy, where it must reliably explode or do whatever else it is designed to do.

Perhaps saddest of all are weapons such as the Tiger tank, which were in many ways paragons of excellence but were simply too complex and expensive to manufacture to be available in useful numbers.

Left: Despite its thin armour and diminutive turret, more than 6000 PzKpfw I tanks served during World War II.

ROMAN REPEATING BALLISTA ANCIENT

Theoretically sound, the repeating ballista was essentially a giant crossbow. It used a magazine of bolts which were loaded using a cam system, allowing rapid shooting.

However, the repeating ballista was very heavy and could not be quickly re-aimed, and was sufficiently accurate to put its bolts into a small area. That meant that astute enemies could observe where the first one went and not be there for the others. Realigning the ballista to a new target was slower than reloading and firing the standard, lighter, version, negating all the advantages of this otherwise clever and workable weapon.

SPECIFICATIONS

TYPE:	Primitive artillery piece
MODE OF OPERATION:	Torsion
PROJECTILE:	Heavy pointed bolt
RANGE:	100m (328ft)
EASE OF USE:	Moderate
COMPOSITION:	Wood and rope, complex
USERS:	Roman army, derived from Greek weapons

The Romans were not great innovators in the field of weaponry, but generally made clever and inventive use of other people's designs (usually the Greeks). This is a late Roman ballista fulminalis, or spear-throwing ballista.

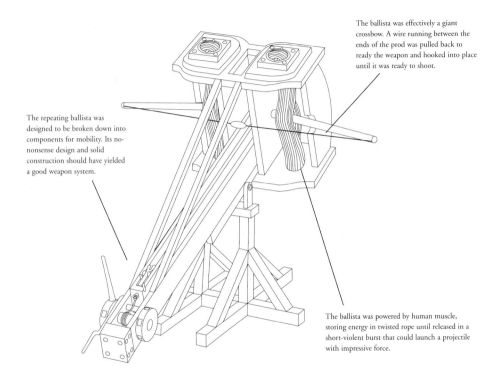

The ballista was effectively a giant crossbow. A wire running between the ends of the prod was pulled back to ready the weapon and hooked into place until it was ready to shoot.

The repeating ballista was designed to be broken down into components for mobility. Its no-nonsense design and solid construction should have yielded a good weapon system.

The ballista was powered by human muscle, storing energy in twisted rope until released in a short-violent burst that could launch a projectile with impressive force.

MODEL 1877 FIELD GUN 1877

Short of artillery weapons, the Italian Army in World War I dug a number of Model 1877 Siege Guns out of storage and attempted to use them as field weapons, without any real success.

The gun's 149.1mm (6in) shells imposed a huge logistics requirement, and the gun had no traverse system at all, meaning that the whole five-ton weapon had to be manually dragged round to a new bearing. In addition, there was no recoil system; the entire gun ran backwards up a set of wooden wedges and rolled back down. Accurate firing was thus somewhat problematical.

The terrain in Italy is hilly where it is not mountainous, and what the Italian army really needed was light mountain howitzers rather than these huge impediments. Trench warfare also required high-angle firing, and these weapons were not suited to that either. They would most likely have been just as useful if left in storage.

SPECIFICATIONS

TYPE:	Artillery piece
CALIBRE:	149.1mm (6in)
WEIGHT:	5180kg (11,400lb)
BARREL LENGTH:	3.42m (11ft)
EFFECTIVE RANGE:	900m (2950ft)
PAYLOAD:	30kg (80lb) high explosive
USERS:	Italy

The Italians also placed great reliance on other heavy weapons, such as this 300-mm (11.8-in) gun, but their lack of mobility was a hindrance when the Central Powers broke through.

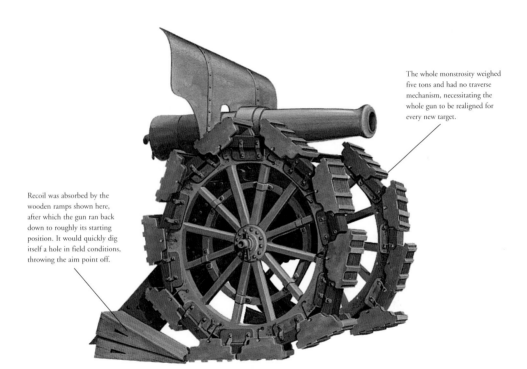

The whole monstrosity weighed five tons and had no traverse mechanism, necessitating the whole gun to be realigned for every new target.

Recoil was absorbed by the wooden ramps shown here, after which the gun ran back down to roughly its starting position. It would quickly dig itself a hole in field conditions, throwing the aim point off.

SIMS-DUDLEY DYNAMITE GUN 1885

A rather novel artillery piece using compressed air to launch a dynamite charge at its target, the Sims-Dudley Dynamite Gun was prone to jam, and when it did so clearing the gun was a lengthy process. It had an effective range of under 1000m (3280ft), meaning that the crew were within rifle shot of their targets much of the time. Given that dynamite can sometimes be set off by a bullet impact, this was not a good thing. The dynamite gun also used a high trajectory and thus the charge was prone to being blown off target by strong winds.

SPECIFICATIONS

TYPE:	Artillery piece powered by compressed air
LENGTH:	4.25m (14ft)
CALIBRE:	62.5mm
PAYLOAD:	2.4kg (5lb) nitro-glycerine
EFFECTIVE RANGE:	900m (2950ft)
COMPLEXITY:	Low
USERS:	Military (USA)

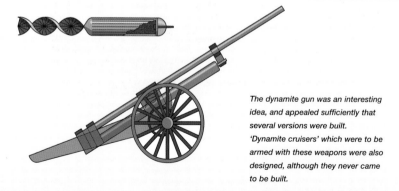

The dynamite gun was an interesting idea, and appealed sufficiently that several versions were built. 'Dynamite cruisers' which were to be armed with these weapons were also designed, although they never came to be built.

Using compressed air to launch a dynamite charge, the Sims-Dudley design was a most interesting idea.

Working around a live dynamite charge was not a popular pastime.

In addition to its short range, it tended to jam, requiring a lot of work to clear it.

SEABROOK ARMOURED CAR 1915

Developed for use by the Navy, the Seabrook Armoured Car mounted a three-pdr (47mm) gun as main armament and either two or four machine guns, all in a heavily armoured chassis that was more akin to a battleship than a useful light armoured vehicle.

Despite some interesting features such as sides that could be lowered to allow the main gun a better field of fire (which incidentally deprived the crew of their protection!), the Seabrook was too overloaded and could operate only on good roads. Even there, it would sometimes suffer suspension problems and even broken axles. An armoured vehicle that cannot move is definitely not much of an asset.

SPECIFICATIONS

TYPE:	Armoured reconnaissance vehicle
DIMENSIONS:	7.3x2.1x1.8m (24x7x6ft)
SPEED:	32km/h (20mph)
ARMOUR:	8mm maximum
ARMAMENT:	1 x 47mm gun plus 2–4 .303 machine guns
CREW:	6
USERS:	Britain

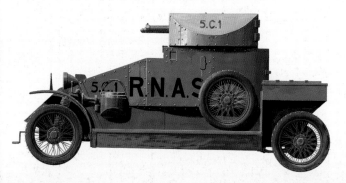

The more conventional and altogether more successful Lanchester armoured car, a contemporary of the Seabrook. Motorized transport was in its infancy and failed experiments were inevitable.

More gunboat than armoured vehicle, the Seabrook had good protection for the driver and engine, but was badly overloaded.

The sides of the Seabrook could be lowered to improve the field of fire for the main and secondary armament.

SIZAIRE-BERWICK ARMOURED CAR 1915

The Sizaire-Berwick Wind Wagon was a most interesting vehicle created by Royal Air Force personnel. Driven by a propeller powered by an aero engine on the back of the vehicle, it had novelty on its side at least. However, with an unprotected radiator and engine, it could be easily put out of action by enemy fire. The single .303 machine gun was limited to a narrow forward arc, though the two-man crew was well protected in an armoured box.

Sizaire-Berwick seems to have been the air force's answer to the Seabrook. If the navy wanted to build a warship with wheels, the air force would respond with a ground-borne fighter aircraft.

SPECIFICATIONS

TYPE:	Armoured reconnaissance vehicle
DIMENSIONS:	Probably 6x2x1.8m (19x6ft 6inx6ft)
SPEED:	Unknown
ARMOUR:	Minimal
ARMAMENT:	1 x .303 machine gun
CREW:	2
USERS:	Britain

The contemporary French Model 1915 armoured car, while primitive in appearance, was somewhat more practical. It mounted a 37mm gun and an 8mm machine gun.

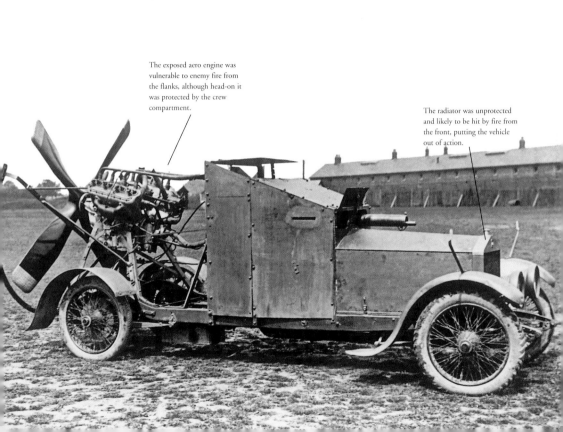

The exposed aero engine was vulnerable to enemy fire from the flanks, although head-on it was protected by the crew compartment.

The radiator was unprotected and likely to be hit by fire from the front, putting the vehicle out of action.

EARLY BRITISH TANKS *1916*

T he first tanks were crude and clumsy affairs that required a large crew to operate. They were relatively mobile and carried a useful armament of either six-pdr guns or machine guns into action while protecting the crew reasonably well.

However, a tank was a hellish environment. It was noisy, hot and stressful inside, and crews were frequently injured by spallation – armour fragments shaken loose by enemy fire. There was also the possibility of being trapped in a burning tank or being riddled with enemy fire whilst stuck and unable to move. The biggest problem was reliability. Far more tanks broke down than were destroyed by enemy action.

SPECIFICATIONS (Mk1 Tank)

TYPE:	Armoured combat vehicle
DIMENSIONS:	8x4.1x2.5m (26x13x8ft)
SPEED:	6km/h (4mph)
ARMOUR:	12mm (½in) maximum
ARMAMENT:	2 six-pdr guns or machine guns
CREW:	8
USERS:	Britain

Obviously designed with trench crossing in mind, the British Mk1 tank was an unreliable monster that broke down at the slightest opportunity. Despite this, it achieved considerable success and demonstrated that the tank was a viable concept.

'Little Willie', shown here, was not so much a combat vehicle as a technology demonstrator. It served its purpose, which was to show that a tracked armoured vehicle was a possibility.

The vehicle was steered using trailing wheels, with help from the tracks. This system was used in early tanks until track-only steering became more viable.

Tracked vehicles had been in existence for some time. Little Willie used a variant on the Bullock Creeping Grip tracks, a US invention.

CHAR D'ASSAULT ST CHAMOND 1917

Developed independently by the French, the St Chamond carried an impressive armament of one 75mm gun and four machine guns. Upon entry to service in 1916, however, this armoured combat vehicle was discovered to have two rather serious flaws.

The St Chamond was petrol-powered, making it prone to bursting into flames when hit. More seriously, and inexplicably in the age of trench warfare, its body extended well out past the end of its tracks, resulting in an unstable vehicle that became stuck easily in difficult terrain. The decision to convert the surviving examples into resupply carriers was probably a wise one.

SPECIFICATIONS

TYPE:	Armoured combat vehicle
DIMENSIONS:	8.8x7.9x2.67m
SPEED:	(29x26x9ft)
ARMOUR:	8.5km/h (5mph)
ARMAMENT:	17mm (½in) maximum
	1 x 75mm gun and up to
	four machine guns
CREW:	9
USERS:	France

A clumsy 'land-battleship' rumbles along a road near the battle front. The design of the St Chamond defies explanation in an era when the battlefield was dominated by trenches and similar obstacles.

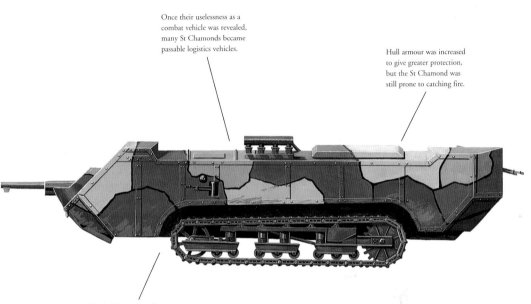

Once their uselessness as a combat vehicle was revealed, many St Chamonds became passable logistics vehicles.

Hull armour was increased to give greater protection, but the St Chamond was still prone to catching fire.

The St Chamond stuck out over the ends of its tracks and was extremely vulnerable to becoming 'ditched'.

STURMPANZERWAGEN A7V 1918

The German contribution to armoured warfare in World War I was the A7V, a gigantic vehicle with slab sides that made an excellent target. Armed with a 57mm gun and six machine guns, the A7V was expensive to manufacture and only 20 were ever fielded. When they reached the battlefield their worst failing was revealed.

With a ground clearance of just 40mm (1½in) and tracks that were shorter than the body, the A7V could not cross rough ground very well. The result was a big slow target that could not keep up with the infantry it was supposed to support.

SPECIFICATIONS

TYPE:	Armoured combat vehicle
DIMENSIONS:	8x3x3.3m (26x10x11ft)
SPEED:	12.9km/h (8mph)
ARMOUR:	30mm (1in) maximum
ARMAMENT:	1 x 57mm gun, six machine guns
CREW:	18
USERS:	Germany

Resembling mobile barns, a group of A7Vs moves up along a road. Offroad performance was poor and the A7V made a big target. The A7V's overcomplexity was destined to be repeated in many World War II German tank designs.

The main armament of one 57mm gun was impressive, although the A7V had difficulty bringing its armament to bear.

Huge slab sides made the tank an easy target and although its armour was reasonable for the time, it was still fairly vulnerable to enemy fire.

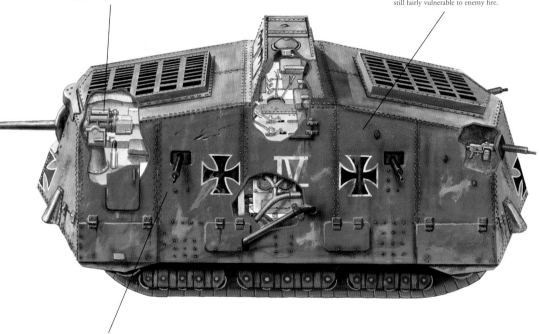

Most of the crew manned the main gun, with the others distributed throughout the enormous vehicle.

TYPE 89 GRENADE DISCHARGER 1929

The Japanese Type 89 Grenade Discharger was actually not a bad weapon, just misunderstood. Essentially a light 50mm (2in) infantry mortar, it could be carried by infantrymen and provide a measure of self-support capability using indirect fire. It became a bad weapon when Allied forces captured some and mistranslated its name as 'knee mortar'.

Various attempts to use the 'knee mortar' braced against the firer's legs (or actually resting on them) resulted in broken limbs and also grenades flying off at random to the detriment of all concerned.

SPECIFICATIONS

TYPE:	Infantry support weapon
CALIBRE:	50mm
WEIGHT:	4.7kg (10lb)
BARREL LENGTH:	254mm (10in)
EFFECTIVE RANGE:	650m (2,132ft)
PAYLOAD:	800g (28oz) grenade
USERS:	Japan

A US infantryman experiments with the Type 89. It was not designed to be fired resting on a man's legs, but a mistranslation resulted in many attempts. Used properly it was actually a fairly decent weapon.

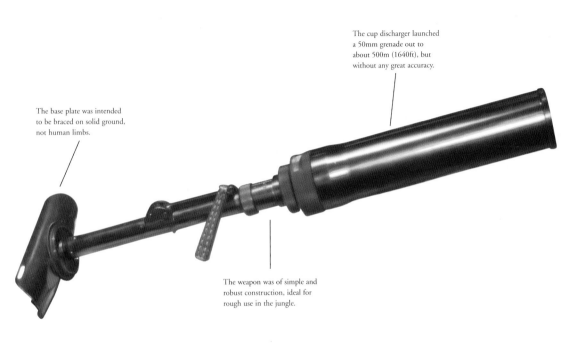

The cup discharger launched a 50mm grenade out to about 500m (1640ft), but without any great accuracy.

The base plate was intended to be braced on solid ground, not human limbs.

The weapon was of simple and robust construction, ideal for rough use in the jungle.

T-35 HEAVY TANK 1933

The T35 heavy tank mounted no fewer than five turrets. Two turrets (one mounting a machine gun and one with a 45mm or 37mm gun) faced forward, a similar pair back, and the main turret with its 76mm howitzer fired over the top of them all.

This impressive array of weaponry was carried in a hull weighing a hefty 45 tons and was protected by a rather thin 10–30mm (½–1in) of armour. It was comparable with medium tanks of the time but hardly impressive. Not only were the guns difficult to coordinate, the tank itself was hard to steer and prone to break down. Before common sense reasserted itself in the 1930s, 61 were built.

SPECIFICATIONS

TYPE:	Heavy armoured combat vehicle
DIMENSIONS:	9.7x3.2x3.4m (32x10ft 6inx11ft)
SPEED:	30km/h (19mph)
ARMOUR:	30mm (1in) maximum
ARMAMENT:	1 x 76mm howitzer, 2 x 45 or 37mm guns, six 7.62mm machine guns
CREW:	11
USERS:	Russia

The T-35 looked fearsome in parades in Moscow and probably impressed everyone who did not actually have to fight aboard them. Although multi-turreted tanks were briefly popular in the 1930s, they faded from the scene quickly when actual combat broke out.

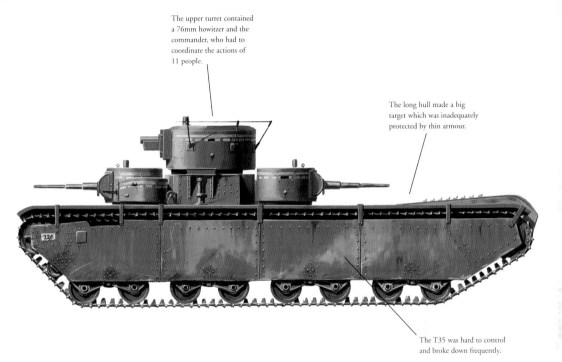

The upper turret contained a 76mm howitzer and the commander, who had to coordinate the actions of 11 people.

The long hull made a big target which was inadequately protected by thin armour.

The T35 was hard to control and broke down frequently.

PZKPFW I LIGHT TANK 1934

The PzKpfw I was never intended to be a serious combat vehicle. Designed as a training tank, it mounted a small turret containing a pair of machine guns and had some limited capability as a reconnaissance vehicle. However, the need for numbers of tanks in the new Panzer formations meant that more than 6000 PzKpfw I were built and formed the backbone of the German armoured formations in the early war years.

Much has been made of the invincibility of the Panzer divisions, but in fact they were mostly armed with these inadequate vehicles, which were by no means bad – just out of their element and doing the best they could.

Light tanks on exercise in the 1930s. The PzKpfw I was intended as an interim training vehicle to permit crews to operate real tanks when they became available. It ended up filling in for those real tanks.

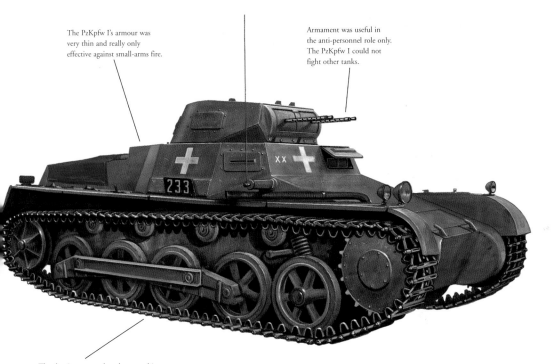

The PzKpfw I's armour was very thin and really only effective against small-arms fire.

Armament was useful in the anti-personnel role only. The PzKpfw I could not fight other tanks.

The chassis was sound, and was used in specialist vehicles long after the PzKpfw I was withdrawn from combat duty.

TYPE 95 HA-GO LIGHT TANK 1935

Armed with a 37mm gun and two machine guns, one facing backwards, the Type 95 had the tools to get the job done, but suffered from too many defects. Its firepower was reduced by the fact that the commander had to fire the gun and the very poor visibility afforded the crew. It could be rendered entirely impotent by a brave soldier armed with a knife – the turret could be jammed with any suitable object. On top of all this, the armour was so thin that antitank rounds would go through both sides and carry on; the Type 95 could sometimes be disabled with a machine gun.

SPECIFICATIONS

TYPE:	Light armoured combat vehicle
DIMENSIONS:	4.38x2x2.18m (14x6ft 6inx7ft)
SPEED:	45km/h (28mph)
ARMOUR:	12mm (½in) maximum
ARMAMENT:	1 x 37mm gun, two machine guns
CREW:	3
USERS:	Japan

This Type 95 is warlike enough in appearance, but it is something of a paper tiger. The Type 95 would not have survived in Europe, but in the Pacific theatre it was able to perform despite its weaknesses.

The main gun was a reasonable weapon, but was hampered by the way it was operated.

The Ha-Go's paper-thin hull armour was entirely inadequate even for a light tank.

The Type 95's only virtue was that it was there – other powers thought that tanks could not operate in the jungle, and the Ha-Go was largely unopposed by its more competent peers.

TYPE 89B MEDIUM TANK 1935

The Type 89B was a reasonable design at inception, but it was obsolete by the time war broke out. With little protection, it was designated a medium tank and mounted a 57mm gun plus two machine guns.

The Type 89's main drawback was that the crew were virtually blind to their surroundings and had to work in very cramped quarters, which reduced efficiency. The tank was also somewhat underpowered and unmanoeuvrable, and when deployed to Manchuria its diesel engine was found to be intolerant of cold weather.

SPECIFICATIONS

TYPE:	Armoured combat vehicle
DIMENSIONS:	5.73x2.13x2.56m
	(19x7x8ft)
SPEED:	26km/h (16mph)
ARMOUR:	17mm (⅝in) maximum
ARMAMENT:	1 x 57mm gun, 2 x
	6.5mm machine guns
CREW:	4
USERS:	Japan

Type 89Bs wearing branches as camouflage. Despite operational problems in the cold of Manchuria, Type 89s were reasonably effective in that theatre. When they came up against European troops in the Pacific, their defects were thrown into sharp relief.

The short 57mm gun was a reasonable weapon, but awkward to serve. Acquiring or even spotting targets could be problematical.

The turret was very cramped, with poor all-round visibility. This made the Type 89 vulnerable to infantry attack in close terrain.

The Type 89 was also difficult and tiring to drive, and not very manoeuvrable.

MATILDA I INFANTRY TANK 1936

The British A11, or 'Matilda', tank possessed extremely good armour that could easily defeat most projectiles. Mechanically it was very reliable, with a good suspension and many other fine features. It should have been a world-class weapon.

The designers, however, fitted the Matilda I with a completely inadequate armament of one machine gun. The result was a very durable tank that could shoulder aside virtually any opposition to reach its target … but could not do anything useful when it got there. The Matilda I was mostly used as a training tank after the Dunkirk evacuation; a shame for such a durable machine with such promise.

SPECIFICATIONS

TYPE:	Armoured combat vehicle
DIMENSIONS:	4.85x2.29x1.87m
	(16x7ft 6inx6ft)
SPEED:	13km/h (8mph)
ARMOUR:	60mm (2¼in) maximum
ARMAMENT:	1 x .303 machine gun
CREW:	2
USERS:	Britain

A Matilda II unloads from a transporter. The mark II version mounted a 40mm (two-pdr) gun and was altogether more effective. It served with distinction throughout World War II.

The Matilda I was hard to kill, but could not contribute effectively to a battle. Its well-armoured turret housed only a machine gun.

The basic design of the Matilda was excellent and represented a lot of wasted effort to bring such an inadequate weapon system to the battlefield.

Designed with infantry support in mind, perhaps for a refight of World War I, the Matilda had good trench-crossing capabilities.

SKODA TANKETTE 1936

Tankettes – essentially, miniature tanks – were popular between the World Wars for some reason. While they had some merit as training and infantry support vehicles, the military value of tankettes was always rather limited. Nevertheless, various companies built and marketed them, and buyers could always be found.

The Skoda S-1 Tankette was one such offering. Armed with a pair of 7.92 machine guns and capable of slightly outpacing a running man on level terrain, it carried a crew of two and was 'protected' by armour too thin to stop small-arms fire. It was thus effectively an underarmed deathtrap for the crew.

SPECIFICATIONS

TYPE:	Light combat vehicle
DIMENSIONS:	3x1.85x1.3m (10x6x4ft)
SPEED:	42kph (26mph)
ARMOUR:	15mm (½in) maximum
ARMAMENT:	2 x 7.92 machine guns
CREW:	2
USERS:	Romania, Yugoslavia

The fearsome shape of the Skoda tankette. Many nations (such as Poland) had few real tanks and tried to make up numbers with these entirely inadequate vehicles. Their main value was the ability to act as a mobile machine-gun emplacement.

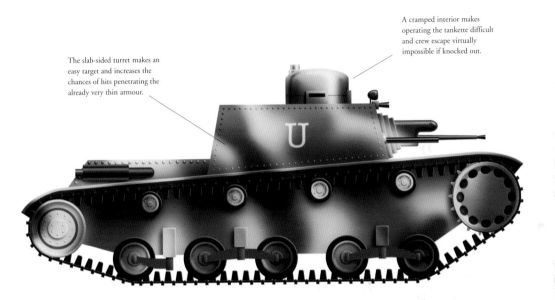

A cramped interior makes operating the tankette difficult and crew escape virtually impossible if knocked out.

The slab-sided turret makes an easy target and increases the chances of hits penetrating the already very thin armour.

U

M11/39 MEDIUM TANK *1939*

I talian tank design in World War II left a lot to be desired. Realizing that their CV33 tanks were a failure, the Italians followed with a new design, the M11/39, which was in the same vein. Armed with a 37mm gun and two machine guns, the M11/39 was underarmoured and high-sided. This made it a big target – always a liability in a tank and especially in desert warfare where there was little cover to be had. Only 100 M11/39s were built. They were sent to North Africa in 1940, where the British destroyed most of them.

SPECIFICATIONS

TYPE:	Armoured combat vehicle
DIMENSIONS:	4.73x2.18x2.3m
	(15ft 6inx7x8ft)
SPEED:	33km/h (20.5mph)
ARMOUR:	30mm (1in) maximum
ARMAMENT:	1 x 37mm gun, 2 x 8mm
	machine guns
CREW:	3
USERS:	Italy

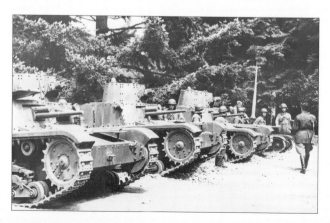

M11/39s lined up for inspection. While an improvement on earlier designs, the M11 was inadequate for the role it was thrust into and suffered accordingly.

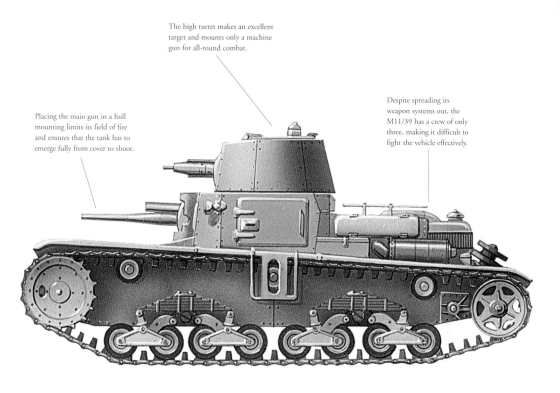

The high turret makes an excellent target and mounts only a machine gun for all-round combat.

Despite spreading its weapon systems out, the M11/39 has a crew of only three, making it difficult to fight the vehicle effectively.

Placing the main gun in a hull mounting limits its field of fire and ensures that the tank has to emerge fully from cover to shoot.

CONVERTED MODEL 1914 INFANTRY GUNS 1939

Finland's involvement in World War II is often forgotten, but in fact some desperate fighting took place there. Faced with the prospect of invasion by tank-heavy enemy forces and needing an effective counter, the Finns redesignated a number of 37mm infantry guns (light artillery pieces) as antitank weapons and deployed them, some to front-line units.

Known as the 37 K/15, this weapon was totally useless in its new role. Its short barrel – designed to give it added mobility in the infantry support role – meant that the muzzle velocity was too low to do much damage.

Other nations fielded successful 37mm antitank guns, but these were designed for the role and could fire a solid penetrator round at high velocity on a flat trajectory. This weapon could not penetrate the armour of the lightest Russian tanks, even from very close range. Its chances of surviving long enough to get a shot off at this distance were extremely slim.

SPECIFICATIONS

TYPE:	Antitank gun
CALIBRE:	37mm
WEIGHT:	90kg (198lb)
BARREL LENGTH:	1m (3ft)
EFFECTIVE RANGE:	250m (820ft)
PENETRATION:	10mm (1/2in)
USERS:	Finland

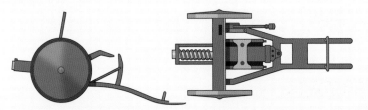

Rather than being adapted for their new use as antitank weapons, these light infantry guns were merely redesignated and sent out to do their pathetic best.

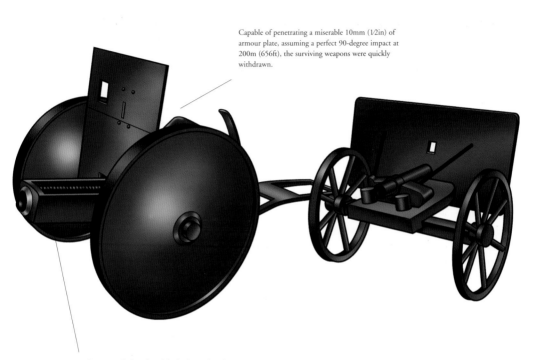

Capable of penetrating a miserable 10mm (1/2in) of armour plate, assuming a perfect 90-degree impact at 200m (656ft), the surviving weapons were quickly withdrawn.

Antitank guns need a long barrel for high muzzle velocity. This gun had a short barrel to improve its mobility in the infantry-support role.

L-35/36 ANTITANK MACHINE GUN 1939

Finland's quest for an effective antitank weapon also included the deployment of a handful of 13mm machine guns. These could be converted into a semi-automatic antitank rifle, although at 35kg (77lb) it was rather heavy.

Some examples made it into combat, where they underperformed rather spectacularly. Even at just 30m (98ft), the L-35 could not penetrate the armour of a T-26 light tank from any direction. In addition, the weapon was not capable of handling the Finnish winter. Tested in summer, it had functioned well enough (apart from its dismal penetration characteristics) but in winter it simply froze up and stopped working. This seems like a curious oversight for a country such as Finland.

Other nations managed to build anti-tank rifles and posed at least a marginal threat to the target in calibres down to 7.92mm. Thus the concept of a 13mm anti-tank weapon is not entirely without basis in reality. What let this weapon down was the fact that it was a conversion of an already poor weapon into a role it was never intended to fill. Some examples retained automatic fire capability and were therefore at least useful for infantry support – at least, when they were not frozen solid.

SPECIFICATIONS

TYPE:	Antitank gun
CALIBRE:	13mm
WEIGHT:	70kg (154lb) with carriage
RATE OF FIRE:	500 rpm
EFFECTIVE RANGE:	250m (820ft)
PENETRATION:	10mm (⅖in) at 100m (328ft)
USERS:	Finland

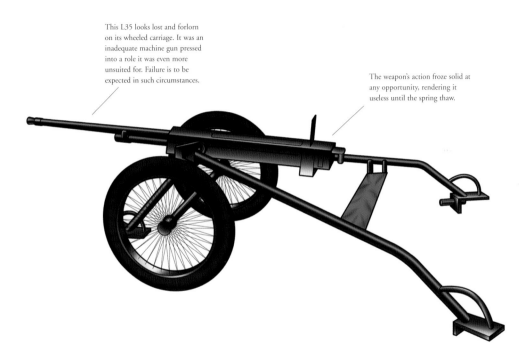

This L35 looks lost and forlorn on its wheeled carriage. It was an inadequate machine gun pressed into a role it was even more unsuited for. Failure is to be expected in such circumstances.

The weapon's action froze solid at any opportunity, rendering it useless until the spring thaw.

T-100 HEAVY TANK 1939

As late as 1938, some Russian tank designers were obsessed with multiple turrets. The T-100 heavy tank was conceived with three turrets and eventually built with two. The 75mm main gun sat in a main turret, while a 45mm gun was carried in a separate turret forward. Three machine guns were also mounted.

The T-100 needed a large crew and, while better protected than the T-35, it was also heavier. On combat trials in Finland it proved useless and the design was scrapped. An experimental version mounting a 130mm main gun was tried, and actually fought in the defence of Moscow, but this was not pursued either.

SPECIFICATIONS

TYPE:	Heavy armoured combat vehicle
DIMENSIONS:	7.4x3.2x3.2m (24x10ft 6inx10ft 6in)
SPEED:	35km/h (22mph)
ARMOUR:	70mm (3in) maximum
ARMAMENT:	1 x 75mm gun, 1 x 45mm gun, 3 machine guns
CREW:	7
USERS:	Russia

A T-100 heavy tank pretending to be a battleship. The T-100 was a big, high-sided target. While less insane than most other multi-turret tanks, the project was abandoned. No successful multi-turret fighting vehicles have ever emerged.

The main gun would have been more effective with a longer barrel, but the second turret necessitated a shorter, lower-velocity weapon.

The front turret's 45mm gun was probably more effective against enemy armour than the main gun. It was mounted low, however, and was thus restricted.

The T-100 required a big crew, a long hull and a lot of power to carry its armament into battle. Better returns were to be had from more modest vehicles.

SIG 33 SELF-PROPELLED GUN *1940*

Experience in Poland showed the German army that a self-propelled gun was needed, and so the SIG 33 was born. A hurried design, it consisted of a 150mm (6in) artillery piece in a very high-sided mount armoured to the front and sides. The gun was mounted whole, complete with its wheels and trail, adding to the load that the chassis had to carry.

The resulting monstrosity was difficult to operate due to cramped conditions around the gun. It also had very limited ammunition stowage, little traverse and it made a big target. The SIG 33 was quickly withdrawn from service as better replacements became available.

SPECIFICATIONS

TYPE:	Self-propelled artillery
DIMENSIONS:	4.67x2.06x2.8m
	(15x6ft 8inx9ft)
SPEED:	40km/h (25mph)
ARMOUR:	13mm (½in) maximum
ARMAMENT:	1 x 150mm gun
CREW:	4
USERS:	Germany

A SIG33 in the field. An innovation thrown together in response to battlefield experience, it filled a need – more or less – until better custom-designed weapons were available.

128

The SIG33 made use of existing hardware and mounted a very large gun, but at the price of carrying a lot of weight.

Perching a field artillery piece on top of an armoured chassis presented few engineering or design challenges, but it was not an elegant solution.

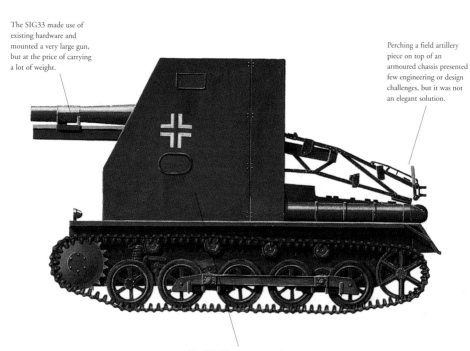

The SIG 33's armour was a token gesture, offering a little protection from small-arms fire to the crew.

STUKA-ZU-FUSS (FOOT STUKA) 1940

By bolting a number of Wurfkörper artillery rockets in wooden cases to the outside of a SdKfz 251 half-track, the German army attempted to turn it into a fire support vehicle. The resulting contraption, referred to as the 'Howling Cow' or 'Foot Stuka', delivered considerable though rather random firepower.

The rockets were aimed by pointing the vehicle and were less than accurate, and coming under fire with half a dozen very large bombs strapped to the vehicle body was an unpleasant experience. En masse, the 'Foot Stuka' was capable of devastating an area, but on the whole it was not a very good system due to its inherent inaccuracy.

SPECIFICATIONS

TYPE:	Self-propelled fire-support system
DIMENSIONS:	5.8x2.1x1.75m (19x6ft 9inx5ft 8in)
SPEED:	52km/h (32mph)
ARMOUR:	14.5mm (⅝in) maximum
ARMAMENT:	6 x artillery rockets, 1 x 7.92 machine gun
CREW:	2
USERS:	Germany

The improvised nature of the Foot Stuka can be clearly seen from this picture. The danger posed by the rockets when hit by enemy fire or even just colliding with something was considerable.

The Foot Stuka used the existing (and successful) SdKfz 251 half-track as its basis. Once the rockets were gone the vehicle continued to be useful in its infantry-carrying role, and no doubt the crew breathed a bit easier, too.

The rockets were carried in wooden frames, which were often very crude.

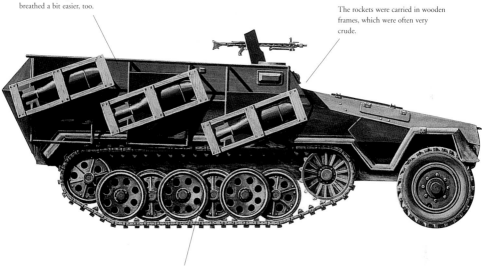

Sometimes the frames were set at different angles to spread a salvo out, but the inherent inaccuracy of the rockets usually accomplished that anyway.

T-60 LIGHT TANK *1941*

The Soviet army of World War II liked light tanks, despite growing evidence that they were ineffective. Redesigning the unsuccessful T-40, they created the T-60, which was supposedly better than its predecessor. It was intended to scout for the medium and heavy tanks, and support them in combat.

Mounting a 20mm gun, the T-60 could not fight other tanks and in any case its pathetic armour (only 7mm/¼in in many areas) served only to prevent the crew escaping when their vehicle was inevitably disabled. On top of that, the wholly inadequate engine could not provide enough mobility to keep up with the T-34s of the battle formations.

SPECIFICATIONS

TYPE:	Light armoured combat vehicle
DIMENSIONS:	4.11x2.3x1.74m (13ft 5inx7ft 6inx5ft 8in)
SPEED:	45km/h (28mph)
ARMOUR:	25mm (1in) at thickest point
ARMAMENT:	1 x 20mm cannon, 1 x 7.62mm machine gun
CREW:	2
USERS:	Russia

A propaganda photograph showing a command conference around a T-60 light tank. Supposedly a reconnaissance vehicle for the tank formations, the T-60 was little more than a liability on the battlefield.

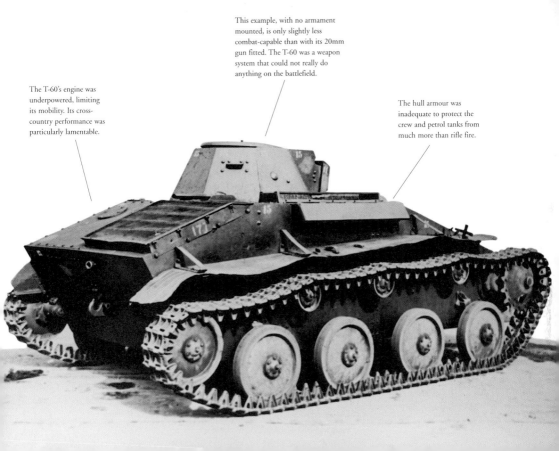

The T-60's engine was underpowered, limiting its mobility. Its cross-country performance was particularly lamentable.

This example, with no armament mounted, is only slightly less combat-capable than with its 20mm gun fitted. The T-60 was a weapon system that could not really do anything on the battlefield.

The hull armour was inadequate to protect the crew and petrol tanks from much more than rifle fire.

KV-II HEAVY TANK 1940

The KV-I was an effective heavy combat vehicle with good armour and a powerful gun, but the KV-II was less good. Designed as an 'artillery tank' mounting a 152mm howitzer in a high-sided turret, the KV-II shared a general lack of reliability with the KV-I, but had some new problems of its own. The turret was so badly designed that it could traverse fully only on level ground. The KV-II was also underpowered for its weight and not very mobile. While this tank was hard to kill and so useful in defensive operations, it could not cope with fast-paced offensives of the sort that characterized the later war years.

SPECIFICATIONS

TYPE:	Armoured support vehicle
DIMENSIONS:	6.8x3.3x3.65m (22x10ft 9inx12ft)
SPEED:	25km/h (15.5mph)
ARMOUR:	110mm (4in) maximum
ARMAMENT:	1 x 152mm gun, 3 machine guns
CREW:	6
USERS:	Russia

A knocked-out KV-II with a BA-10 armoured car in the foreground. The KV-II's gun was of a sound design and potentially a useful weapon system. It was the tank as a whole that was a failure.

The high turret made a good target. Fortunately it was heavily armoured, although its mounting to the chassis left a lot to be desired.

The KVII used the KVI chassis, the reliability issues of which were not resolved in the new version.

The overall vehicle was useful as a self-propelled artillery piece, but in a fluid mobile battle it was ineffective.

PZKPFW VI TIGER I HEAVY TANK 1942

The Tiger I quickly gained a reputation as a deadly opponent due to its heavy armour and powerful 88mm main gun. The Tiger was not, however, quite the ultimate weapon it seemed. Hugely expensive to produce and rather complex to maintain, the Tiger absorbed a lot of resources in return for its formidable combat power. Just getting it to the battlefield presented a problem.

The Tiger was too heavy for most bridges and a lot of roads, and the running gear suffered from clogging in muddy conditions. Its gun was immensely powerful, but traversed very slowly, and its performance in the field was hampered by being underpowered and fuel-greedy.

SPECIFICATIONS

TYPE:	Heavy armoured combat vehicle
DIMENSIONS:	8.45x3.56x3m (28x11ft 7inx9ft 9in)
SPEED:	37km/h (23mph)
ARMOUR:	100mm (4in) maximum
ARMAMENT:	1 x 88mm gun, 2 or 3 x 7.62mm machine guns
CREW:	5
USERS:	Germany

Tiger Is in the field. The Allies rightly feared the mighty gun of the Tiger and it was well protected, making it hard to kill. In a strategic sense, however, the Tiger was to prove a failure.

The Tiger's distinctive slab sides made penetration slightly more likely, but its heavy armour was still very formidable.

The Tiger's engine was inadequate and also fuel-greedy, creating logistics problems.

The running gear was a weakness; the overlapping road wheels clogged easily.

The Maus was so heavy it could not reach its design speed of 20km/h (12mph), nor could it use any bridge then in existence. It could crawl around at about 13km/h (8mph) on the flat. With its coaxial 128mm and 75mm guns, the Maus might have been formidable on the defensive or perhaps moving slowly forward as a mobile artillery emplacement, but as an armoured combat vehicle it was a total failure.

The project was scrapped in 1944, although work was continued on the prototypes. Two were complete at the end of the war.

SPECIFICATIONS

TYPE:	Superheavy armoured combat vehicle
DIMENSIONS:	10.09x3.67x3.66m (33ftx12x12ft)
SPEED:	13km/h (8mph)
ARMOUR:	200mm (8in) maximum
ARMAMENT:	1 x 128mm gun, 1 x 75mm gun, 1 x 7.96mm machine gun
CREW:	5
USERS:	Germany

Two Maus prototypes and most of a third were intact at the end of World War II. There was at one point a plan to fit out one Maus for the final defence of Berlin. It would have made no difference to the outcome, but such a last stand might have partially justified all the wasted development work.

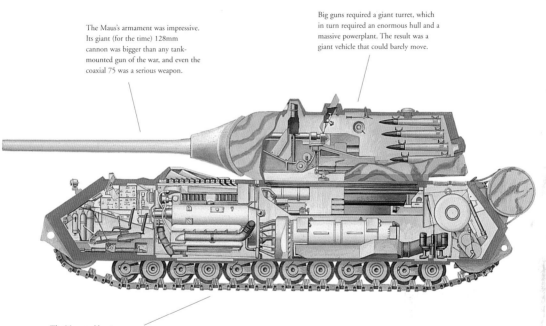

The Maus's armament was impressive. Its giant (for the time) 128mm cannon was bigger than any tank-mounted gun of the war, and even the coaxial 75 was a serious weapon.

Big guns required a giant turret, which in turn required an enormous hull and a massive powerplant. The result was a giant vehicle that could barely move.

The Maus could not cross any bridge in Germany, so great was its weight.

TYPE 4 SELF-PROPELLED GUN 1943

Feeling the need for self-propelled artillery support late in the Pacific war, the Japanese army mounted an obsolete 5.9mm howitzer (which dated from 1905 and had already been withdrawn from service as a field piece) on the chassis of the Type 97 light tank.

The result was a short-ranged, thinly armoured and generally inadequate vehicle with a very slow rate of fire due to the design of the original gun. Type 4s were then deployed in tiny numbers across various islands where they entirely failed to contribute to the defence effort.

In the face of massed bombardment by rockets and conventional tube artillery plus aircraft and, often, naval guns of up to 400mm (16-inch) calibre, the Type 4 was utterly insignificant. There were simply too few of them to make any difference even if they had been a half-decent weapon system – which they were most certainly not.

SPECIFICATIONS

TYPE:	Self-propelled artillery
DIMENSIONS:	5.3x2.3x1.5m (17ft 5inx7ft 6inx5ft)
SPEED:	38km/h (23mph)
ARMOUR:	25mm (1in) maximum
ARMAMENT:	1 x 150mm Howitzer
CREW:	4 or 5
USERS:	Japan

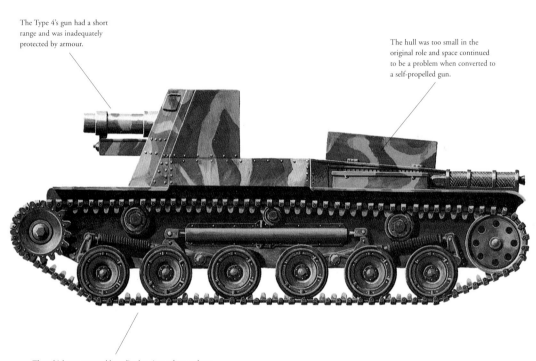

The Type 4's gun had a short range and was inadequately protected by armour.

The hull was too small in the original role and space continued to be a problem when converted to a self-propelled gun.

The vehicle was powered by a diesel engine and was at least less flammable than its petrol-powered contemporaries. This was the Type 4's main virtue.

M4 SHERMAN 'DD' *1944*

The DD, or Duplex Drive, Sherman tank suffered from all the same problems as the standard version – weak armour and a tendency to catch fire so pronounced that they were nicknamed 'Ronson Lighters' after a brand with the slogan 'First time, every time'. The Duplex Drive Sherman suffered from the additional problem that it thought it could swim.

By erecting a flotation screen and engaging the secondary propeller drive, the Sherman DD could theoretically be deployed into water and advance onto a beach under its own power. Unfortunately, many vehicles sank during the D-Day landings, killing the crews before they could even get ashore.

SPECIFICATIONS

TYPE:	Amphibious armoured combat vehicle
DIMENSIONS:	5.88x2.68x2.74m (19x8ft 9inx9ft)
SPEED:	39km/h (24mph)
ARMOUR:	62mm (2½in) maximum
ARMAMENT:	1 x 75mm gun, 1 x .50 machine gun, 2 x 7.62mm machine gun
CREW:	5
USERS:	USA

A Sherman DD with flotation screen erected. In completely calm water the DD was able to manoeuvre adequately, but even then entering the water was a fraught business. In rough water it was extremely dangerous.

Nervous crewmembers cling to the frame as the tank enters the water. Note how calm the sea is.

Once in the water, the propeller drive will propel the tank shorewards, although currents may cause serious problems.

LCT 4

BTR-152 ARMOURED PERSONNEL CARRIER 1950

A six-heeled vehicle that entered Soviet service in the 1950s, the BTR-152 borrowed some German and US ideas to create a fairly poor vehicle with very limited cross-country performance.

Up to 14 infantrymen could ride in the troop compartment, protected from the sides and rear but exposed by the open top to shell fragments, NBC weapons and, of course, the weather. They could fire their weapons through ports in the sides, but the chances of hitting anything whilst moving cross-country were slim. Although the BTR-152 was not very good, at least it was cheap, and some examples remain in service around the world.

SPECIFICATIONS

TYPE:	Armoured personnel carrier
DIMENSIONS:	6.83x2.32x2.05m (22x7ft 7inx6ft 8in)
SPEED:	75km/h (46mph)
ARMOUR:	12mm (½in) maximum
ARMAMENT:	1 x .50 machine gun or 1 x 7.62mm machine gun
CREW:	2
USERS:	Russia, Warsaw Pact countries, overseas buyers

Basically just a light armoured truck, the BTR-152 was one of the earliest armoured personnel carriers to enter service. It has been built in vast numbers and examples are still encountered worldwide.

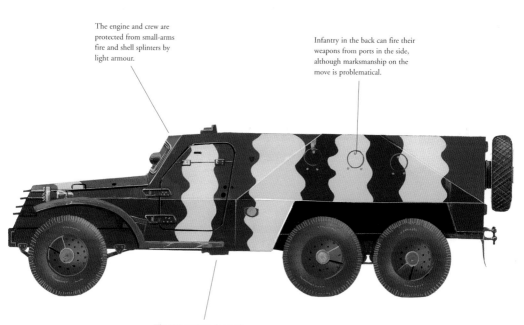

The engine and crew are protected from small-arms fire and shell splinters by light armour.

Infantry in the back can fire their weapons from ports in the side, although marksmanship on the move is problematical.

The BTR-152's good ground clearance affords it reasonably good cross-country performance, while wheeled design keeps costs down.

M-65 ATOMIC HOWITZER 1951

Only one actual nuclear round is known to have been fired from a cannon. The weapon was a US M-65 'Atomic Annie' 280mm cannon. The gun delivered a 15-kt nuclear shell to a target range some 11km (seven miles) away.

Twenty M-65s were built by the United States. Weighing 88 tons, the atomic howitzer is not very mobile and requires engineering vehicles to bulldoze it a path if it must manoeuvre off road. This, combined with a relatively limited range, made the M65 relatively useless except in static bombardment or if it could be placed in the path of an enemy offensive, where it ran the risk of being overrun.

SPECIFICATIONS

TYPE:	Nuclear artillery weapon
CALIBRE:	280mm (11in)
WEIGHT:	83 tons
BARREL LENGTH:	14m (45ft)
EFFECTIVE RANGE:	30km (19 miles)
PAYLOAD:	280mm high explosive or 15-kt nuclear
USERS:	USA

In the one and only test-firing undertaken with a live nuclear shell, the M-65 Atomic Howitzer successfully delivers its payload. At the time many people feared that this was an image of wars to come, but thus far sanity has prevailed.

The 280mm howitzer was equivalent to many World War II railway guns. These were of fairly limited utility, but did play a minor part in the war.

When not launching a nuclear payload, the M-65 could fire a large high-explosive shell, but this was not worth the effort in getting the gun into range.

Such a big weapon required a huge carriage to support it, and this greatly reduced mobility.

ONTOS TANK DESTROYER 1955

The M50 Tank Destroyer was conceived as a light vehicle that could be air-transported, offering anti-armour capability with its six 106mm recoilless rifles. Given that it reached the battle area by air, resupply could pose a problem. Even if the six weapons were carried loaded, ONTOS could carry just 18 rounds, which had to be reloaded manually from outside the vehicle. Firing the guns created a huge backblast that no enemy could fail to notice, and the ONTOS was not well armoured enough to survive much in the way of counterfire. After a brief period of service ONTOS was quietly retired and forgotten about.

SPECIFICATIONS

TYPE:	Tank destroyer
DIMENSIONS:	3.83x2.6x2.13m
	(12ft 6inx8ft 6inx7ft)
SPEED:	48km/h (30mph)
ARMOUR:	13mm (½in) maximum
ARMAMENT:	6 x 106mm recoilless rifles,
	1 x 7.62mm machine gun
CREW:	3
USERS:	USA

A gunner reloads a tube aboard an Ontos tank destroyer, a dangerous occupation in proximity to the enemy. Early in the Vietnam War, rules of engagement required that the Ontos secure Battalion-level permission before loading or firing its weapons, so loading in the field was almost a certainty.

The six 106mm recoilless rifles were poor antitank weapons, but the Marines discovered a use for them, firing 'beehive' rounds like a giant shotgun.

The crew compartment was very cramped, making the Ontos difficult to operate. Its name means 'thing' in Greek.

The Ontos prototype was built around a proven chassis and later versions retained many of its good features. The Ontos was at least manoeuvrable.

M113 ARMOURED PERSONNEL CARRIER 1956

An armoured personnel carrier in use with the US and many other armed forces, the M113 is not without its drawbacks, despite its success. The use of aluminium armour means that if an M113 catches fire it will burn fiercely and the blaze will be very difficult to extinguish. With a petrol engine aboard this was not good news; more recent versions have a diesel engine.

Defensively the M113 is not great. The thin armour can be penetrated by armour-piercing rounds and widely available rocket-propelled grenades. Early versions had no protection for the commander when using the machine gun, leading to needless casualties.

SPECIFICATIONS

TYPE:	Armoured personnel carrier
DIMENSIONS:	2.52x2.69x1.85m
	(8x8ft 9inx6ft)
SPEED:	61km/h (37mph)
ARMOUR:	45mm (2in) maximum
ARMAMENT:	1 x .50 machine gun
CREW:	2
USERS:	USA, many overseas buyers

The M113 has been adopted by a great many armed forces and serves as the basis for a range of variants, from field ambulances and command posts to air-defence vehicles and tank destroyers. Basing variants on a common chassis simplifies maintenance greatly.

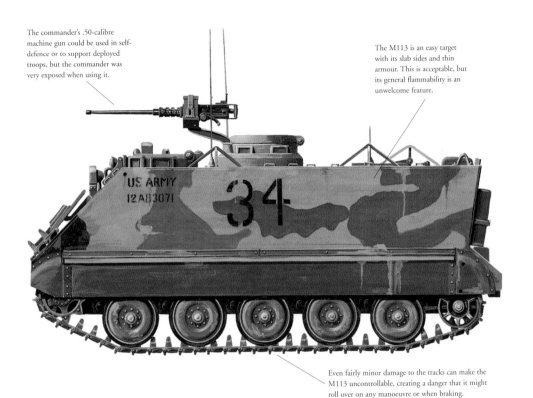

The commander's .50-calibre machine gun could be used in self-defence or to support deployed troops, but the commander was very exposed when using it.

The M113 is an easy target with its slab sides and thin armour. This is acceptable, but its general flammability is an unwelcome feature.

Even fairly minor damage to the tracks can make the M113 uncontrollable, creating a danger that it might roll over on any manoeuvre or when braking.

M551 SHERIDAN LIGHT TANK 1960

The Sheridan was another victim of the appalling Shillelagh weapon system. Not only did early Shillelagh systems cause cracked gun barrels, but also firing the gun/launcher in gun mode fouled the barrel and disrupted the electronics so that the missile no longer worked properly.

Even when the missile capability was dropped, the Sheridan still had problems. These included a tendency to explode when hit due to the nature of its ammunition. On top of that, firing the gun made the tank hop into the air, damaging electronic components inside, and the Sheridan was so lightly armoured that even a heavy machine gun posed a threat to it.

SPECIFICATIONS

TYPE:	Light armoured combat vehicle
DIMENSIONS:	6.3x2.82x2.95m (20ft 7inx9x9ft 7in)
SPEED:	72km/h (45mph)
ARMOUR:	Light
ARMAMENT:	1 x 152mm gun/missile system, 1 x 7.62mm machine gun
CREW:	4
USERS:	USA

The Sheridan was a good idea – an air-mobile vehicle capable of killing tanks and fulfilling other support roles. It was let down, however, by a terrible weapon system. The resulting vehicle was all but useless for anything except distracting enemy fire from more useful assets.

The Shillelagh gun/missile system was a disaster which ruined more than one otherwise promising vehicle design.

The Sheridan was highly mobile and could go almost anywhere. Unfortunately there was little it could do when it got there.

The Sheridan's protection was simply too thin for serious combat. It looks like a tank and attracts antitank weapons, but can be killed by a machine gun.

153

The W-54 'Davy Crockett' was a man-portable 'nuclear bazooka' capable of delivering a small nuclear warhead. It could be mounted on a light vehicle or fired by infantry from a tripod. The name 'Davy Crockett' suggests that this was a weapon of desperation to be used in a last-stand situation.

The Davy Crockett was successfully trialled in 1962 and about 400 were in service during the next decade. With a lethal radiation radius of about 350m (1150ft) and a minimum range of about 400m (1312ft), the W-54 could pose something of a hazard to its users, and there is something just not quite right about infantry-launched nuclear weapons.

SPECIFICATIONS

TYPE:	Nuclear delivery system
CALIBRE:	120mm or 155m
WEIGHT:	30kg (66lb)
LENGTH:	76cm (30in)
EFFECTIVE RANGE:	120mm version: 2km (1 mile), 155mm version: 4km (2.5 miles)
PAYLOAD:	W54 tactical nuclear warhead
USERS:	USA

A W54 battlefield nuclear warhead. In the 1950s it was more or less expected that any future major war would be fought with nuclear munitions. The enemy hordes would be halted by a wall of mushroom clouds. Thus far, this unpleasant vision has been incorrect.

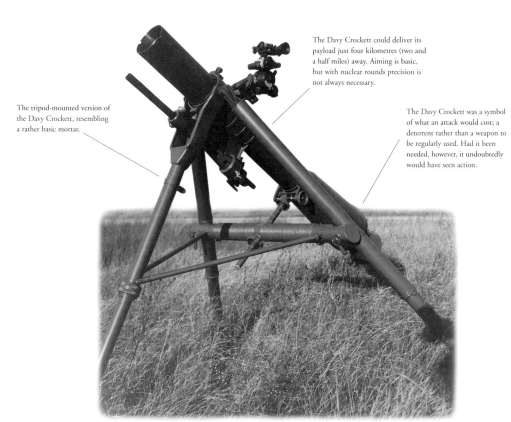

The Davy Crockett could deliver its payload just four kilometres (two and a half miles) away. Aiming is basic, but with nuclear rounds precision is not always necessary.

The tripod-mounted version of the Davy Crockett, resembling a rather basic mortar.

The Davy Crockett was a symbol of what an attack would cost; a deterrent rather than a weapon to be regularly used. Had it been needed, however, it undoubtedly would have seen action.

AMX-30 MAIN BATTLE TANK 1963

The AMX-30 had its origins in discussions between France, Germany and Italy in the 1950s. Over 1200 were delivered to the French army and the chassis was used as the basis for a range of other vehicles. Armed with a 120mm gun and a coaxial 20mm cannon, the AMX-30 seems quite potent.

However, the emphasis on speed and cross-country performance meant that the AMX-30 was somewhat under-armoured and vulnerable. During the 1991 Gulf War, the main armoured drive was undertaken by US and British armoured formations, with the French in a supporting role. It seems that the Coalition commanders felt the AMX-30 too lightly protected to undertake a spearhead role.

SPECIFICATIONS

TYPE:	Armoured combat vehicle
DIMENSIONS:	9.48x3.1x2.29m (31x10x7ft 6in)
SPEED:	65km/h (40mph)
ARMOUR:	80mm (3in) maximum
ARMAMENT:	1 x 105mm gun, 1 x 20mm cannon, 1 x 7.62mm machine gun
CREW:	4
USERS:	France, Spain, Cyprus, Greece, Venezuela, Saudi Arabia

In use with several armed forces, the AMX-30 is a commercial success, but is not quite in the same class as the Abrams and Challenger tanks it served alongside in the Gulf War. The more recent Leclerc remedies many of its deficiencies.

The 105mm main gun is outdated; most modern MBTs use a 120mm weapon.

The AMX-30's armour is thin by MBT standards, limiting its survivability.

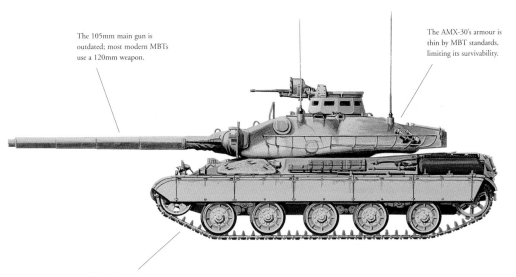

Although emphasis was placed on speed and agility, the AMX-30 is not outstanding in that field.

TYPE 63 SELF-PROPELLED AA GUN 1963

China needed a self-propelled anti-aircraft weapon and had a large number of ex-Soviet T34 tank chassis available. It seemed simplicity itself to mount a tall, open-topped turret on the chassis and mount a pair of 37mm guns in it.

And that is exactly what the Type 63 is. Two guns sitting in a turret. It cannot mount radar of any sort and is manually elevated, so cannot track a fast aircraft. Even if it could, its manually reloaded five-round clips severely limit its firepower and ability to obtain hits. For some reason this inadequate weapon was kept in service until almost 1990.

SPECIFICATIONS

TYPE:	Self-propelled anti-aircraft weapon
DIMENSIONS:	6.43x2.99x3m (21x9ft 9inx9ft 9in)
SPEED:	55km/h (34mph)
ARMOUR:	45mm (1¾in) maximum
ARMAMENT:	2 x 37mm cannon
CREW:	6
USERS:	China, some overseas clients including Vietnam and Korea

China obtained a lot of military equipment from the Soviet Union before relations deteriorated. Much of China's equipment was built to or derived from these designs, and the influence can still be seen today.

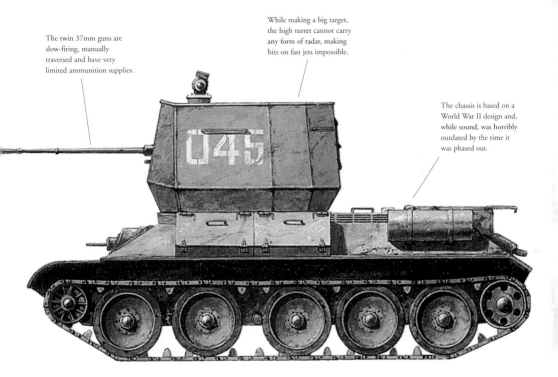

The twin 37mm guns are slow-firing, manually traversed and have very limited ammunition supplies.

While making a big target, the high turret cannot carry any form of radar, making hits on fast jets impossible.

The chassis is based on a World War II design and, while sound, was horribly outdated by the time it was phased out.

M60A2 MAIN BATTLE TANK *1964*

The M60 Main Battle Tank was a powerful and effective fighting vehicle. Armed with a 105mm gun, it could deal with most threats. The A2 version, however, was a different story.

Equipped with the Shillelagh gun/missile system, the M60A2 was not a success, mainly due to problems with the weapon system. Although it seemed like a good idea to give tanks a guided weapon system, the Shillelagh was badly flawed and fitting it to the M60 was akin to removing its teeth. Shillelagh rendered the M60 impotent, and most M60A2s were quickly converted to bridgelayers or engineering vehicles.

SPECIFICATIONS

TYPE:	Armoured combat vehicle
DIMENSIONS:	9.44x3.63x3.27m
	(31x12x10ft 8in)
SPEED:	48km/h (30mph)
ARMOUR:	143mm (6in) maximum
ARMAMENT:	1 x 105mm gun, 1 x .50
	machine gun, 1 x 7.62mm
	machine gun
CREW:	4
USERS:	USA, Israel, overseas buyers

A vision of air–land battle. Armoured vehicles supported by helicopter gunships would smash the enemy and exploit their breakthroughs ruthlessly. The toothless M60A2 was capable of contributing absolutely nothing to such a battle except its own burning wreckage.

The awful Shillelagh gun/missile system that crippled the Sheridan also ruined the M60A2.

Without a decent gun, the M60A2's array of advanced sensors was a waste of money.

The basic design was sound; a fine tank ruined by a useless weapon.

FROG-7 1965

The FROG (Free Rocket Over Ground) series of missile launchers were designed for short-range battlefield support. FROG-7 can deliver a nuclear, chemical or conventional round, albeit rather inaccurately, over a distance of about 70km (44 miles). Introduced in 1965, FROG-7 was finally replaced by somewhat better systems starting in the middle of the 1970s.

The main problem with FROG-7 is its inaccuracy, which makes using it with conventional warheads fairly useless. The standard FROG erector-launcher provides no NBC protection for the crew, which for a weapon designed to be used with nuclear and chemical warheads can be a problem.

SPECIFICATIONS

TYPE:	Unguided heavy artillery rocket system
CALIBRE:	550mm
WEIGHT:	22 tons
ROCKET LENGTH:	9.1m (30ft)
EFFECTIVE RANGE:	70km (43 miles)
PAYLOAD:	450kg (992lb) high explosive or 5-kt or 25-kt nuclear or chemical warhead
USERS:	Russia, Warsaw Pact countries, some overseas buyers

A FROG-7 and its crew assembled for inspection. The Warsaw Pact deployed large numbers of these weapons, allowing the delivery of large warheads more or less at random ahead of the advancing tank armies. This was a fairly pointless exercise without chemical or nuclear munitions, which would result in a response in kind.

The FROG-7 erector-launcher could move to the firing point, launch, then slip away, hopefully evading retribution.

The common Soviet deployment was in battalions of four launchers, with supporting and command vehicles.

Launch preparation takes 15–30 minutes, but reloading takes longer and requires a crane.

SPARTAN TANK DESTROYER *1978*

The MILAN-armed tank destroyer version of the Spartan vehicle falls short of expectations due to its inadequate weapon system. The MILAN antitank guided missile is very good, but it is an infantry weapon. In infantry hands it gives good service, but when mated to the Spartan the result is a large target equipped with a weapon that is vastly outranged by the tanks it is supposed to fight, and without the protection it needs to survive. MILAN cannot engage targets at much over 2km (1.2 miles), as compared to the 4-km (2.4-mile) range of the missiles carried by the US Bradley, which is not a dedicated tank destroyer.

SPECIFICATIONS

TYPE:	Tank destroyer
DIMENSIONS:	5.13x2.24x2.26m
	(17x7ft 3inx7ft 5in)
SPEED:	80km/h (50mph)
ARMOUR:	Light
ARMAMENT:	1 x MILAN missile
	launcher, 1 x 7.62mm
	machine gun
CREW:	3
USERS:	UK

The MILAN missile launcher was designed for infantry use, rather than installation on top of a tracked vehicle.

The weapon system is an infantry MILAN missile launcher, which lacks the range for serious antitank combat aboard a vehicle.

Cross-country performance is excellent, giving the Spartan a fighting chance to get into position for an ambush.

The Spartan chassis is based on the Scorpion light tank and is very good indeed.

165

SERGEANT YORK 1983

Sergeant York was intended to bring powerful anti-air firepower to the forward battle area. In the event it proved unable to track low-flying targets like the helicopters it was supposed to deal with, and it could not traverse fast enough to hit a crossing target anyway. On top of that its radar tended to pick up its own gun barrels when searching for higher-flying targets, its ECM suite was virtually useless and the M48 chassis was outdated, meaning that the vehicle could not keep up with the armoured assets it was designed to protect. Other than that, the project was a success.

SPECIFICATIONS

TYPE:	Self-propelled anti-aircraft weapon
DIMENSIONS:	7.67x3.63x4.61m (25x12x15ft)
SPEED:	48km/h (30mph)
ARMOUR:	120mm (4¾in) maximum
ARMAMENT:	2 x 40mm cannon
CREW:	3
USERS:	USA

A Sergeant York DIVAD (Divisional Air Defence) vehicle on trials. The very prominent radar antennae look the part, but the vehicle's radar suite was very poor, making the whole project an expensive failure even without taking into consideration all its other faults.

Turret traverse was too slow to track a crossing target.

The guns themselves were sound, but without adequate direction they could not perform their designed role.

Sergeant York was unable to keep pace with the vehicles it was designed to protect. This alone made it useless.

AIRCRAFT AND MISSILES

Air warfare is a relatively new concept, and an area where experimentation is constant. Like the ocean, the air is not a tolerant medium, and a weapon that fails may well end its days in a large hole in the ground.

Technology has moved fast in the realm of air war, and many entirely workable drawing-board concepts have been overtaken by events or entered service too late to achieve any useful results. In other cases, complacency or political factors have allowed obsolete weapons to remain in service, with terrible consequences for the crews that had to take them belatedly to war.

Some weapons overcame their teething troubles to become useful, such as attempts to use the excellent Mosquito fighter/bomber to carry a heavy gun for tank-busting duties. Recoil from the weapon caused the aircraft's wings to come off in one experiment, but despite this a version of the weapon system made its way to the battlefield and proved useful. This kind of against-the-odds success is perhaps what encourages development teams to persevere with obviously doomed concepts.

Left: *The Douglas X-3 Stiletto might have looked the part, but it turned out to be a high-speed research vehicle that couldn't go supersonic.*

ZEPPELIN BOMBERS 1915

Zeppelins made useful reconnaissance platforms, especially at sea, but as attack aircraft they left something to be desired. Despite this the raids continued throughout World War I. About once a fortnight raiding airships crawled across the skies to drop a handful of bombs on London, Paris and other significant targets.

About 90 per cent of the bombs missed, and overall the raids were unsuccessful. A single lucky hit caused more than half the damage inflicted by all the Zeppelin raids in the entire war, and the cost of building the airship fleet was about five times greater than the damage they inflicted.

SPECIFICATIONS

TYPE:	Airship bomber
CREW:	Varied
ARMAMENT:	Bombs plus defensive machine guns
RANGE:	Probably around 600km (373 miles)
SPEED:	80km/h (50mph)
BOMB LOAD:	5 tons
USERS:	Germany

The wreckage of a shot-down Zeppelin bomber. Downing a Zeppelin was a difficult task, but if it could be induced to burn, it was doomed. The challenge of defeating Zeppelins absorbed a lot of resources. Given the minimal damage they did, it might have been more cost-effective to ignore them.

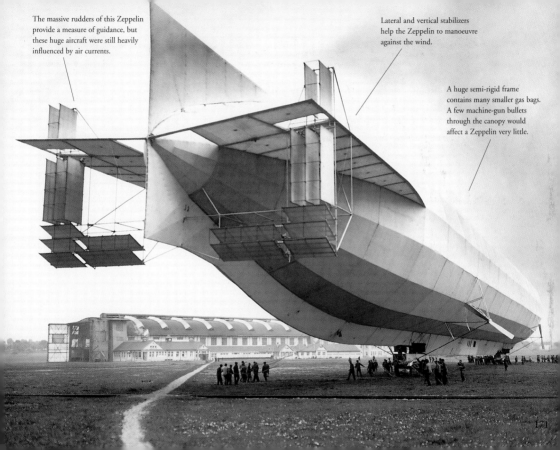

The massive rudders of this Zeppelin provide a measure of guidance, but these huge aircraft were still heavily influenced by air currents.

Lateral and vertical stabilizers help the Zeppelin to manoeuvre against the wind.

A huge semi-rigid frame contains many smaller gas bags. A few machine-gun bullets through the canopy would affect a Zeppelin very little.

171

GOTHA BOMBERS *1916*

German Gotha bombers carried out several raids against targets in Britain during World War I, despite the limitations of the aircraft. Slow and very susceptible to damage, Gothas had a tendency to break their own undercarriage on landing; special runways were laid to help prevent this.

Several models of Gotha appeared and although they improved it was not a good aircraft. A Mk. V Gotha could carry 330kg (727lb) of bombs all the way to London – if it did not get lost or break down on the way. In May 1917, 23 Gothas set out and just two reached the target area. More were lost to operational accidents than to enemy action.

SPECIFICATIONS

(MK V)

TYPE:	Long-range bomber
CREW:	3
ARMAMENT:	Two or three 7.92mm machine guns
RANGE:	850km (525 miles)
SPEED:	140km/h (90 mph)
BOMB LOAD:	550kg/1200lb (330kg/727lb to London)
USERS:	Germany

Once airborne, the Gotha was a fairly decent aircraft, if slow and vulnerable to being shot down. It was on landing and takeoff that its weaknesses were revealed.

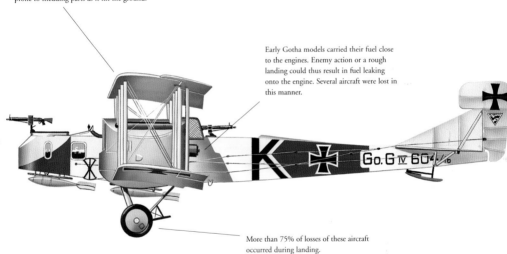

The Gotha's wings had to be redesigned as the original aircraft was both unstable and rather prone to shedding parts as it hit the ground.

Early Gotha models carried their fuel close to the engines. Enemy action or a rough landing could thus result in fuel leaking onto the engine. Several aircraft were lost in this manner.

More than 75% of losses of these aircraft occurred during landing.

HANDLEY-PAGE HEYFORD 1933

The spectacularly ugly Heyford was the RAF's last biplane bomber, entering service in 1933. Obsolete when they entered service, Heyfords were easy to maintain and pleasant to fly, so were popular with their crews. It will never be known if they were any use in combat.

Heyfords saw service as gunnery trainers and testbeds for various equipment, including radar. Fortunately, they never went to war, although the last Heyford squadrons were still operational in 1939. The design was declared obsolete in 1941, about 15 years later than it should have been.

SPECIFICATIONS

TYPE:	Heavy bomber
CREW:	4
ARMAMENT:	4 Lewis machine guns
RANGE:	500km (310 miles)
SPEED:	130km/h (81mph)
PAYLOAD:	1200kg (2645lb) internal
	plus small wing racks
USERS:	Britain

The Handley-Page Heyford in flight. It is indicative of the situation in Europe in the 1930s that Britain was putting Heyfords into service at a time when Germany was developing excellent advanced combat aircraft.

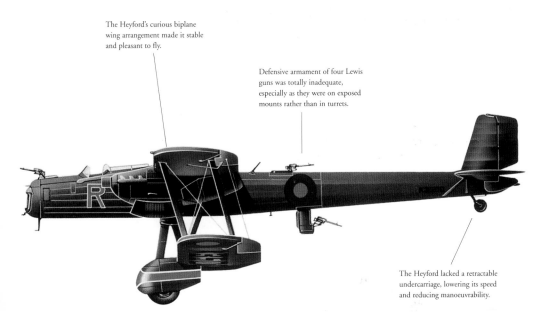

The Heyford's curious biplane wing arrangement made it stable and pleasant to fly.

Defensive armament of four Lewis guns was totally inadequate, especially as they were on exposed mounts rather than in turrets.

The Heyford lacked a retractable undercarriage, lowering its speed and reducing manoeuvrability.

JUNKERS JU 87 STUKA 1936

The Ju-87 was an effective tactical strike aircraft, capable of delivering its bombs accurately at the end of its screaming dive; however, it needed air superiority to survive. Operating in favourable conditions in France, Stukas achieved excellent results, but when sent into the hostile skies over England, where air superiority was anything but guaranteed, they suffered heavy losses.

Many Ju-87s were sent to the Eastern Front or used to attack Malta. There, pilots of the island's fighter defences shot down so many that attacks by Ju-87s were referred to as 'Stuka Parties' and downing one was barely worth calling a 'kill'.

SPECIFICATIONS

TYPE:	Tactical strike aircraft/light bomber
CREW:	2
ARMAMENT:	2 machine guns
RANGE:	800km (497 miles)
SPEED:	310km/h (193mph)
PAYLOAD:	250kg (551lb) (more in later versions)
USERS:	Germany and her allies

The Stuka did its job – delivering bombs – well enough, but it was not survivable in hostile skies. Once it was deprived of air supremacy, the Stuka became much less deadly and suffered heavy losses.

At 300km/h (186mph), the Stuka was not especially fast. This was an asset in accurate bomb delivery, but made the aircraft vulnerable to interception.

If it came to a fight, the pilot had a single forward-firing machine gun with which to attack.

The observer also had a single gun with which to defend the plane. It might have been better to dispense with the gunner/observer and save weight.

FAIREY SWORDFISH 1936

The Fairey Swordfish was a good aircraft in many ways. It could initiate a climbing turn straight off a carrier deck, and its performance remained reliable (if modest) in all conditions. It was, however, horribly outdated when World War II broke out. Plodding along at 220km/h (137mph), the 'Stringbag' was an easy target for enemy fighters and anti-aircraft weapons. The fate of the Swordfishes that attacked German warships during the Channel Dash was grim and predictable.

Yet this was the aircraft that crippled the *Bismarck* and made the daring Taranto raid on the Italian fleet. These successes owed more to the determination of the crews than to the aircraft.

SPECIFICATIONS

TYPE:	Torpedo Bomber/ Maritime Strike Aircraft
CREW:	3
ARMAMENT:	2 machine guns
RANGE:	880km (546 miles)
SPEED:	220km/h (137mph)
PAYLOAD:	1 torpedo or 1 mine or rockets or bombs
USERS:	Britain

A Swordfish lumbers off the flight deck. The 'Stringbag' was outdated and vulnerable, but it was there and it did its best. Some of its exploits are tragic, some heroic, and some a mixture of both. It modestly got the job done, and for that deserves recognition.

The Swordfish's low speed made it vulnerable to anti-aircraft fire as it approached the target.

The gunner's single machine gun was of little use against fast enemy fighters.

Despite its limitations the basic design was sound. The Swordfish's only sin was that it belonged to an earlier era and was obsolete when it was introduced.

5A

ROYAL NAVY
LS326

FAIREY BATTLE 1937

Designed in the early 1930s, the Battle was a single-engined light bomber that entered service in 1937. Slow and weakly armed with a single machine gun fixed forward and another crewed by a rear-facing gunner, Battles were no match for the modern fighters of the Luftwaffe and ground fire found them easy targets. In the early days of World War II, Battles suffered heavy losses as they gallantly tried to oppose the advance of the panzer divisions.

The surviving aircraft were mainly used as trainers, target tugs and experimental testbeds for the remainder of the war.

SPECIFICATIONS

TYPE:	Light bomber/strike aircraft
CREW:	3
ARMAMENT:	2 machine guns
RANGE:	1600km (994 miles)
SPEED:	410km/h (255mph)
PAYLOAD:	440kg (970lb) internal,
	230kg (507lb) external
USERS:	Britain

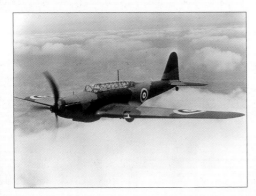

Another product of the 1930s, the Battle was a poor design that was not wanted by its end users. When war broke out, they were forced to do their best with this very poor aircraft, and suffered accordingly. The Battle was withdrawn from active service as quickly as possible.

The Battle was actually a little faster than the Stuka, but not fast enough to survive without air supremacy.

A single rear-firing machine gun was inadequate to defend the aircraft.

Overall performance was rather poor, with a small bomb load.

HEINKEL HE 177 GREIF 1938

Some concepts are doomed from the start. An edict that the new heavy bomber design proposed by Heinkel should also have a dive-bombing capability meant that the four-engined bomber needed to be more aerodynamic. The clever solution of putting pairs of engines in each nacelle did indeed reduce drag, but at the price of a distressing tendency to self-immolate.

Both air and ground crews hated the He 177. Several hundred struggled to cope in a tank-busting role on the Eastern Front, while others attempted dive-bombing attacks over Britain. Neither of these roles was especially suited to a heavy bomber, and most losses were due to engine problems or fires.

SPECIFICATIONS

TYPE:	Heavy/dive bomber
CREW:	6
ARMAMENT:	6 machine guns
RANGE:	5000km (3107 miles)
SPEED:	472km/h (293mph)
PAYLOAD:	6000kg (13,228lb) internal plus torpedoes if carried
USERS:	Germany

An example of the He 177 is pictured here in Allied colours after undergoing a range of tests after World War II.

The Greif was designed to function as a heavy bomber. It was not suited to dive-bombing and functioned badly.

The Greif's clever engine layout reduced drag, but at the price of fires and other losses due to engine malfunctions.

A Greif was converted in Czechoslovakia in readiness to deliver a Nazi atomic bomb. Fortunately the bomb was never manufactured.

VICKERS WELLINGTON *1938*

The massacre of Wellingtons on early raids in World War II demonstrated some serious flaws in the design. The Wellington was not designed to deal with modern cannon-armed fast fighters, and its nose and tail guns could not bear on a target that lay abeam. There was absolutely nothing that gunners could do but traverse their guns to 80 degrees and hope the enemy got careless. The twin .303 machine guns in nose and tail turrets were outranged by many fighter weapons.

Later Wellingtons gained a pair of waist guns, but the design remained very vulnerable to fighter attack, although they were robust and could often get home despite crippling damage.

SPECIFICATIONS

TYPE:	Heavy bomber
CREW:	6
ARMAMENT:	6 machine guns (later 8)
RANGE:	3500km (2175 miles)
SPEED:	410km/h (255mph)
PAYLOAD:	2000kg (4409lb)
USERS:	Britain

The Wellington was an urgently needed replacement for the Heyford. Wellingtons suffered tremendously in the early months of World War II. Had Bomber Command flown the same missions in Heyfords, the results would have been even worse.

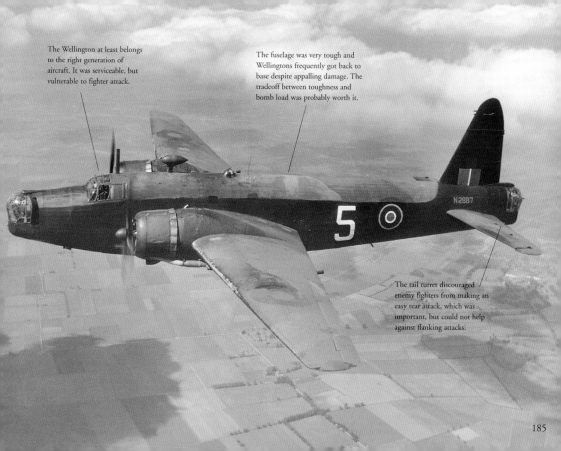

The Wellington at least belongs to the right generation of aircraft. It was serviceable, but vulnerable to fighter attack.

The fuselage was very tough and Wellingtons frequently got back to base despite appalling damage. The tradeoff between toughness and bomb load was probably worth it.

The tail turret discouraged enemy fighters from making an easy rear attack, which was important, but could not help against flanking attacks.

N2887

5

BLACKBURN SKUA 1938

The Skua was designed as a dual-role fighter/dive-bomber. Despite successes such as sinking the German cruiser *Königsberg*, the Skua was not well regarded, and with good cause. It was not the most stable of aircraft. Indeed, its spin characteristics were so bad that a special parachute was added to assist recovery. Speed was not good and rate of climb was very poor.

Although it was a fairly poor aircraft, the Skua was all there was, and it got on with the job at hand. Skuas saw a lot of action and scored some notable successes despite the odds against them.

SPECIFICATIONS

TYPE:	Light bomber/maritime strike aircraft
CREW:	2
ARMAMENT:	4 Browning machine guns, 1 Lewis machine gun
RANGE:	1300km (808 miles)
SPEED:	360km/h (224mph)
PAYLOAD:	1 x 225kg (496lb) bomb
USERS:	Britain

A crash-landed Skua. These inadequate aircraft nevertheless were the first to sink a major warship (the cruiser Königsberg) and the first to carry out an interception guided by shipborne radar.

The gunner/observer also had a single defensive machine gun with which to fight.

The pilot controlled four machine guns, giving the Skua a limited anti-air capability.

Bomb load was modest, with a 250kg (496lb) bomb on the fuselage and light bombs on the wings.

HEINKEL HE 111 *1938*

D esigned under the guise of a civilian transport aircraft, the He 111 served well in the Spanish Civil War and was able to outrun many interceptions. The outcome was very different when the He 111 went up against modern British fighters such as the Hurricane and Spitfire.

Unable to outgun modern fighters and unable to outfight them with its armament of one 20mm cannon, one 13mm machine gun and three 7.92mm machine guns, the He 111 was very vulnerable to interception and large numbers were shot down. However, its credible performance as a bomber and the large numbers already manufactured meant that it was not withdrawn until heavy losses had been suffered.

SPECIFICATIONS

TYPE:	Medium bomber
CREW:	5
ARMAMENT:	Up to 7 machine guns, sometimes one 20mm cannon
RANGE:	2800km (1740 miles)
SPEED:	400km/h (248mph)
PAYLOAD:	2000kg (4409lb) bombs
USERS:	Germany

A crashed He 111. Until it went up against the modern fighters and veteran pilots of the Royal Air Force, the He 111 seemed invincible. It was outmatched, but kept on combat operations for far too long for lack of a replacement and because it had a reputation that took time to destroy.

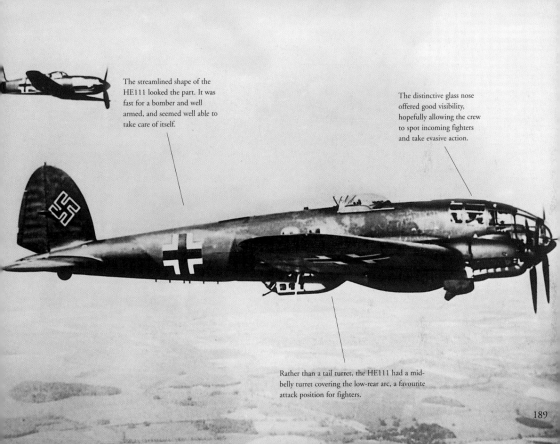

The streamlined shape of the HE111 looked the part. It was fast for a bomber and well armed, and seemed well able to take care of itself.

The distinctive glass nose offered good visibility, hopefully allowing the crew to spot incoming fighters and take evasive action.

Rather than a tail turret, the HE111 had a mid-belly turret covering the low-rear arc, a favourite attack position for fighters.

MESSERSCHMITT BF 209 *1939*

The Messerschmitt Bf 209 was derived from an aircraft designed specifically for high-speed performance. This was not a good basis for a fighter, as, while record-breakers can afford to be temperamental, combat aircraft cannot. Nevertheless, the designers added a cannon and two machine guns, changed the wing design, and began testing.

Whilst very fast, the Bf 209 was a troublesome aircraft with an engine that overheated at any opportunity. Handling was also very poor, an unforgivable flaw in a fighter. After a considerable amount of fiddling about with the design, the team admitted it was a bad job and moved on to something better.

SPECIFICATIONS

TYPE:	Air-superiority fighter
CREW:	1
ARMAMENT:	1 x 20mm cannon, 2 x 7.7mm machine guns
RANGE:	700km (435 miles)
SPEED:	755km/h (469mph)
COMBAT CEILING:	10,000m (32,800ft)
USERS:	Germany

The Bf 209 was an engine with wings, designed to go very fast and not much else. Its performance in a dogfight would be seriously hampered by its poor handling, if it had reached the operational stage at all.

The engine was powerful but prone to problems. Keeping it properly maintained in a fighting squadron would have been a nightmare.

The design favoured speed over handling, which was not a good thing in a fighter aircraft.

The stubby fuselage with cockpit set very far back was necessary to make room for the powerplant. This limited visibility in combat or when landing.

BOULTON-PAUL DEFIANT 1939

The Defiant was a single-engined fighter, with its armament of four machine guns mounted in a turret crewed by a gunner. This added weight, reducing speed and manoeuvrability.

When the machine entered service, its crews soon found that it was impossible for gunners to shoot accurately while the pilot was manoeuvring in a dogfight, unless the pilot flew straight and level to allow his gunner to aim properly. This was a quick and easy way to get killed. The Defiant was thus not a success and was withdrawn from day interceptions, although many went on to do better as radar-equipped night fighters.

SPECIFICATIONS

TYPE:	Air-superiority fighter
CREW:	2
ARMAMENT:	4 x .303 machine guns
RANGE:	750km (466 miles)
SPEED:	490km/h (304mph)
COMBAT CEILING:	12,000m (39,400ft)
USERS:	Britain

The Defiant was an interesting experiment that gave enemy pilots lining up for a rear shot an unwelcome surprise. It soon became apparent, however, that it was not an effective fighter, and its withdrawal from day combat operations was necessitated by heavy losses as the enemy got wise to its capabilities.

Most fighters are vulnerable
in the rear quarter, and most
pilots would try to line up a
shot from this angle. The
Defiant's rear-facing guns
were a nasty surprise.

The overall lines of the Defiant
are reminiscent of the more
conventional Hurricane, which
deceived some enemy pilots.

The Defiant was vulnerable from
underneath and from the front.
Once enemy pilots learned to
distinguish it from other fighters,
it became ineffective.

BLACKBURN ROC *1939*

Another failed turret fighter was the Roc. Derived from the Skua and intended for operation from carriers, the Roc carried four machine guns in a turret behind the pilot. The turret was the same as used in the Defiant, and unsurprisingly the Roc suffered from the same problems.

The Blackburn Roc was a failure as a fighter. Its performance was unimpressive due to weight and drag, and the carrier fleet got rid of it as quickly as possible. The Roc was relegated to a second-line role ashore, where it simply faded from memory as a poor idea, badly implemented.

SPECIFICATIONS

TYPE:	Naval Fighter
CREW:	2
ARMAMENT:	4 x .303 machine guns,
	8 x 15kg (33lb) bombs
RANGE:	990km (615 miles)
SPEED:	315km/h (196mph)
COMBAT CEILING:	4700m (15,420ft)
USERS:	Britain

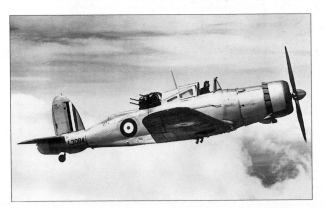

The Blackburn Roc was a carrier-borne fighter with no forward-firing armament. It might have been effective at dealing with enemy long-range reconnaissance aircraft, but against anything faster it was all but useless.

The Roc was underpowered and suffered from drag. It was little faster than a Stuka.

The turret's arc of fire extended to rear and sides, making it difficult to line up an attack on an aircraft that was not flying straight and level.

Like the Defiant, the Roc was vulnerable from in front and underneath. It was not so much a fighter as a flying gun platform.

MESSERSCHMITT BF 110 *1939*

The Bf 110 was conceived as a long-range fighter for patrol and bomber escort work. Equipped with two 20mm cannon plus four machine guns facing forward and a single defensive machine gun pointing aft, it seemed formidable.

When the Me 110 went into combat against Hurricanes and Spitfires in the Battle of Britain, however, it was at a severe disadvantage against these more manoeuvrable aircraft and suffered heavy losses. The only answer was to provide the Me 110 escort fighters with Bf 109 fighters as an escort, which in turn limited the 109s and made them more vulnerable to British fighters.

SPECIFICATIONS

TYPE:	Heavy/escort fighter
CREW:	2
ARMAMENT:	2 x 20mm cannon, 5 x 7.92 machine guns,
RANGE:	2410km (1500 miles)
SPEED:	560km/h (348mph)
COMBAT CEILING:	10,500m (34,500ft)
USERS:	Germany

If looks could kill, the Bf 110 would have been a deadly fighter. Menacing and powerful in appearance, it was based on a flawed concept and could not compete in day combat with single-seaters. The 110 performed better in the night-fighter role.

The distinctive long glassed-in canopy gave good visibility behind and upwards, which was a defensive advantage.

The gunner and his single weapon might better have been dispensed with, lightening the aircraft.

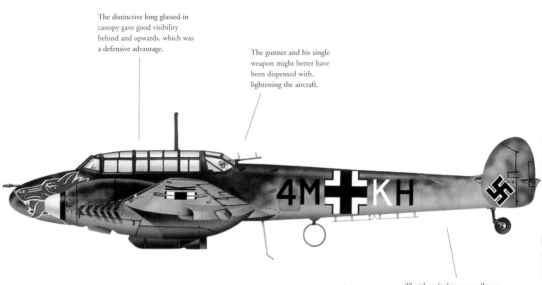

4M✠KH

The idea of a long-range 'heavy fighter' was popular for a while, but the results were never as good as the designers hoped for.

BREWSTER BUFFALO *1939*

The Brewster Buffalo fighter first flew in 1937 and entered service with the US Navy in 1939. When first conceived it was a decent little fighter armed with four machine guns, but it was obsolescent by the time World War II began and suffered accordingly. Performance was highly unimpressive in tests, and in an effort to mitigate this, the armament was reduced from .50 to .303 calibre and the fuel load was restricted. This had obvious implications for combat capability and range.

US Marine Corps Buffaloes deployed to Southeast Asia were massacred by the better equipped and trained Japanese air force, with 15 out of 25 aircraft destroyed. The Finns, to whom 44 aircraft were delivered, had more success, and the type gained a surprising reputation as one of the most successful fighting aircraft ever flown by the Finnish Air Force.

SPECIFICATIONS

TYPE:	Air-superiority fighter
CREW:	1
ARMAMENT:	4 .303 machine guns
RANGE:	1600km (995 miles)
SPEED:	500km/h (310mph)
COMBAT CEILING:	10,000m (32,800ft)
USERS:	USA, Britain, Netherlands, Belgium, Finland and others

A crash-landed Buffalo. These inadequate aircraft were thrown into combat against the Imperial Japanese Air Force, which could deploy some of the best combat aircraft of World War II. They did what they could, but never really stood a chance.

The Buffalo's Wright Cyclone engine could drive it at 500km/h (311mph), only 30km/h (19mph) slower than an A6M Zero. It was less manoeuvrable and outgunned, however.

The short, stubby fuselage made a small target and gave friendly handling characteristics. Many Buffaloes became training aircraft.

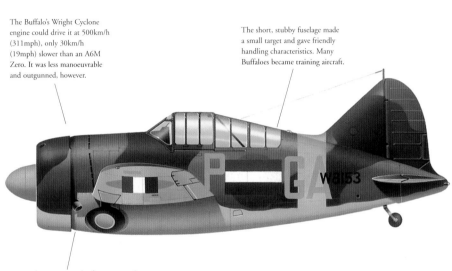

Armament was inadequate, ensuring that the Buffalo was outgunned and outranged by most enemy aircraft.

NORTHROP XP-56 *1940*

The XP-56 was a single-engined monoplane fitted, unusually, with a contra-rotating 'pusher' propeller. Armed with a 20mm cannon and four machine guns, the resulting fighter might have eventually been formidable.

In the event, the XP-56 was difficult to control and tended to yaw at the slightest provocation. Takeoff and landing were especially dangerous as the controls were prone to reversal at low speeds. The magnesium frame was light but burned well, and there were engine difficulties. After losing one prototype and suffering several near-accidents, the USAF decided that this radical design was just too dangerous to fly and scrapped the project.

SPECIFICATIONS

TYPE:	Experimental fighter
CREW:	1
ARMAMENT:	1 x 20mm cannon,
	4 x .50 machine guns
RANGE:	1050km (652 miles)
SPEED:	750km/h (466mph)
WINGSPAN:	13m (42ft 7in)
USERS:	USA

The XP-56 was a most interesting experiment, but experimentation is always fraught with risk. In the case of this aircraft, its problems proved insoluble and the project was cancelled.

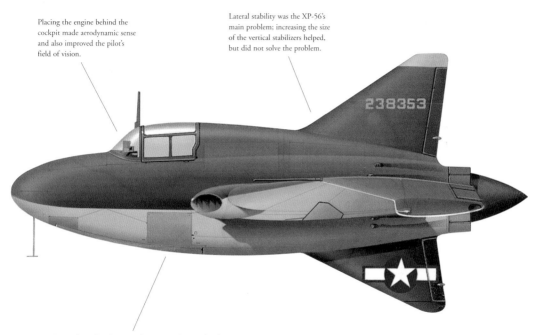

Placing the engine behind the cockpit made aerodynamic sense and also improved the pilot's field of vision.

Lateral stability was the XP-56's main problem; increasing the size of the vertical stabilizers helped, but did not solve the problem.

238353

Despite being based on sound aeronautical principles, the XP-56 was simply too hazardous to keep flying in the hope of ironing out its problems.

BELL P-39 AIRACOBRA 1941

A rather odd design, with the engine mounted behind the pilot to make room for a 37mm cannon in the nose, the Airacobra was more of a turkey than a snake when it entered service. The prototypes had been flown with turbocharged engines, but somewhere in the development process these had been discarded as unnecessary.

Without the turbo, the Airacobra was horribly underpowered and performed very badly. It had a distressing tendency to go into a flat spin. Thus it failed as a fighter and was soon replaced by better designs. However, it gave good service as a low-level attack aircraft and the Russian air force particularly liked it.

SPECIFICATIONS

TYPE:	Fighter/Ground Attack Aircraft
CREW:	1
ARMAMENT:	1 x 37mm cannon, 4 x .50 machine guns, 230kg (507lb) bombs
RANGE:	1770km (1100miles)
SPEED:	600km/h (373mph)
COMBAT CEILING:	10,700m (35,100ft)
USERS:	USA, UK, Russia

The innovative Airacobra might have been a success but for the rather strange decision to remove the turbochargers from its engines. Its weight distribution made it awkward to fly.

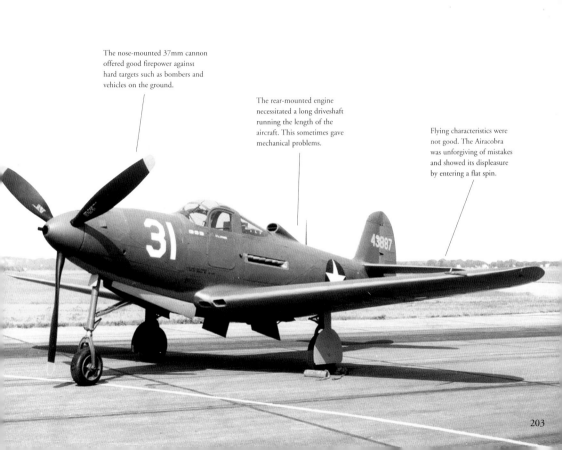

The nose-mounted 37mm cannon offered good firepower against hard targets such as bombers and vehicles on the ground.

The rear-mounted engine necessitated a long driveshaft running the length of the aircraft. This sometimes gave mechanical problems.

Flying characteristics were not good. The Airacobra was unforgiving of mistakes and showed its displeasure by entering a flat spin.

MESSERSCHMITT ME 163 *1943*

The Me 163 'Komet' was a rocket-powered interceptor armed with two 20mm or 30mm cannon. In theory this simple fighter could take off and attack bombers passing overhead, then glide to a landing for re-use.

The Komet's main liability was the propulsion system. Some caught fire or blew themselves up on takeoff or during flight, and a rough landing could cause the remaining fuel to explode. Of all the aircraft lost, only five per cent were due to enemy action. Fifteen per cent lost control or caught fire in the air and the rest exploded on takeoff or landing.

SPECIFICATIONS

TYPE:	Interceptor
CREW:	1
ARMAMENT:	2 x 20mm or 30mm cannon
RANGE:	35km (22 miles)
SPEED:	955km/h (593mph)
COMBAT CEILING:	12,000m (39,400ft)
USERS:	Germany

The Komet was a clever idea for a fast-response interceptor, but it was unsuccessful in practice. Finding pilots for a plane that was more likely to blow itself up than be shot down presented a problem.

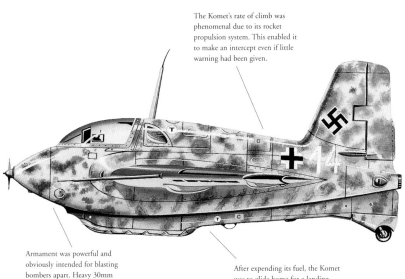

The Komet's rate of climb was phenomenal due to its rocket propulsion system. This enabled it to make an intercept even if little warning had been given.

Armament was powerful and obviously intended for blasting bombers apart. Heavy 30mm cannon are most useful against big targets such as bombers.

After expending its fuel, the Komet was to glide home for a landing. This presented problems for inexperienced pilots. There were few experienced Komet pilots.

SAUNDERS-ROE (SARO) SR.A/1 *1947*

This rather delightful project deserved better success than it achieved. The Saro SR.A/1 was a lightweight single-seat jet powered flying boat fighter. Armed with four 20mm cannon in the nose it was designed in 1943 and intended for service in the Pacific. The end of World War II did away with any real need for such an aircraft and despite a momentary flicker of hope during the Korean War the project was quietly abandoned.

There was absolutely nothing wrong with this aircraft; the prototypes flew and floated as they were intended to do. It was simply not necessary and thus never went into service.

SPECIFICATIONS

TYPE:	Flying boat fighter
CREW:	1
ARMAMENT:	4 x 20mm cannon
SPEED:	825km/h (513mph)
ENDURANCE:	2.4 hours
WINGSPAN:	14m (46ft)
USERS:	UK

The A/1 did everything that was asked of it. Its downfall was that there was simply no need for it by the time development was implemented. Seaplane fighters (perhaps for launch from submarines) have attracted occasional interest, but a production model has never emerged.

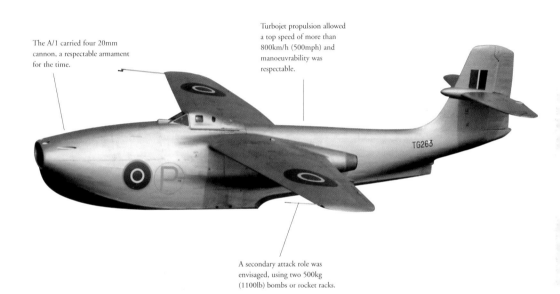

The A/1 carried four 20mm cannon, a respectable armament for the time.

Turbojet propulsion allowed a top speed of more than 800km/h (500mph) and manoeuvrability was respectable.

A secondary attack role was envisaged, using two 500kg (1100lb) bombs or rocket racks.

MISTEL COMPOSITE AIRCRAFT 1943

An ingenious – or perhaps crazy – device intended to get some use out of surplus airframes, the Mistel consisted of a fighter containing the pilot piggy-backed aboard another aircraft packed with explosives. Ju 88s were used for this purpose, along with various other aircraft.

The idea was that the pilot would fly his composite monstrosity towards the target, line it up, then detach his fighter, leaving the pilotless 'missile' to make the attack. Tests were encouraging and some 250 or so Mistels were built, although they never achieved anything significant.

SPECIFICATIONS

TYPE:	Composite aircraft/ piloted missile
CREW:	1
ARMAMENT:	None
RANGE:	1000km (620 miles)
SPEED:	400km/h (248mph)
PAYLOAD:	28,800kg (63,500lb) shaped charge
USERS:	Germany

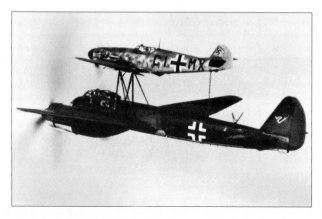

The Mistel concept offered a way to deliver very large explosive charge against precision targets, or so it seemed. In practice, despite considerable effort, negligible damage was caused by Mistel attacks.

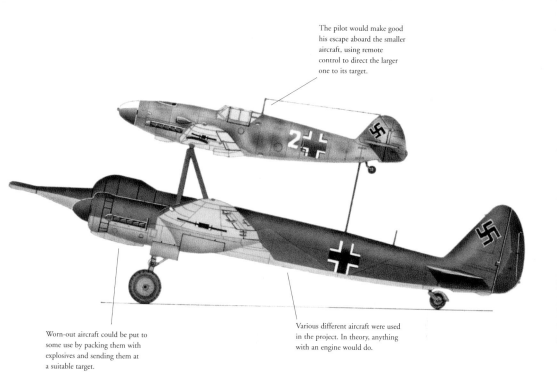

The pilot would make good his escape aboard the smaller aircraft, using remote control to direct the larger one to its target.

Worn-out aircraft could be put to some use by packing them with explosives and sending them at a suitable target.

Various different aircraft were used in the project. In theory, anything with an engine would do.

FIESLER FI 103 REICHENBERG IV PILOTED MISSILE 1944

Attempts to improve the effectiveness of the V1 Flying Bomb included ingenious air-launching schemes. About 1200 V1s were air-launched from converted He111s, though the launch process was a problem and 77 bombers were destroyed in launch accidents. This improved range but did nothing for accuracy, so the idea was formulated to put a pilot aboard in a rudimentary cockpit.

In theory, the pilot was to aim the craft at the target and bale out. However, with no ejector seat, getting out at such a late juncture was a problem. Some pilots were actually willing to perform a kamikaze attack, but most were not, and the project was finally shelved.

SPECIFICATIONS

TYPE:	Piloted missile
CREW:	1
ARMAMENT:	None
RANGE:	250km (155 miles)
SPEED:	650km/h (400mph)
PAYLOAD:	830kg (1800lb) high explosive
USERS:	Germany

The FI 103 is obviously just a V-1 with a cockpit. The official idea was for the pilot to bale out, but a small suicide corps of volunteers (mainly from the thoroughly indoctrinated Hitler Youth) was formed. It was hard to find pilots for one-way missions, however, and in the end the project simply ran out of time.

The 800kg (1764lb) warhead was a powerful weapon if it could be delivered close to the target.

The pilot was supposed to bale out, but a manual ejection at 500–600km/h (310–370mph) was a low-percentage procedure and chances of survival were not good.

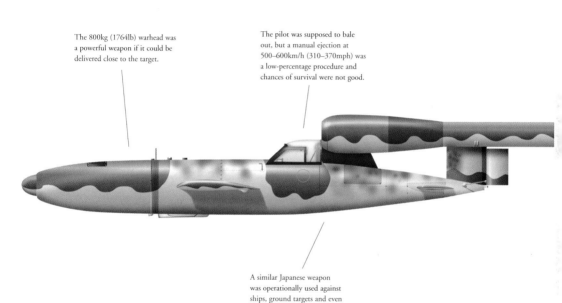

A similar Japanese weapon was operationally used against ships, ground targets and even attacking bombers.

HEINKEL HE 162 'SALAMANDER' 1945

The Salamander was a Volksjäger, or 'People's Fighter', a simple combat aircraft that could be crewed by almost anyone. It was a mostly wooden aircraft powered by a turbojet engine riding piggy-back behind the cockpit. Armament was a pair of 20mm or sometimes 30mm cannon.

The Salamander was not a success. A tendency to crash, plus vibration problems caused by the guns, rendered the finished examples less effective, and endless alterations to the design hampered production of sufficient numbers to be any real use. Given time, the He 162 might have matured into a useful combat aircraft, but events overtook it.

SPECIFICATIONS

TYPE:	Interceptor
CREW:	1
ARMAMENT:	2 x 20mm or 30mm cannon
RANGE:	1000km (620 miles)
SPEED:	900km/h (560mph)
COMBAT CEILING:	12,000m (3280ft)
USERS:	Germany

Designed specifically to make use of materials that were not needed elsewhere, the Salamander was a last-ditch attempt to resist the massive bomber offensives that were rolling across Germany. It was to be crewed by Hitler Youth volunteers and other personnel who were not busy making weapons or manning them.

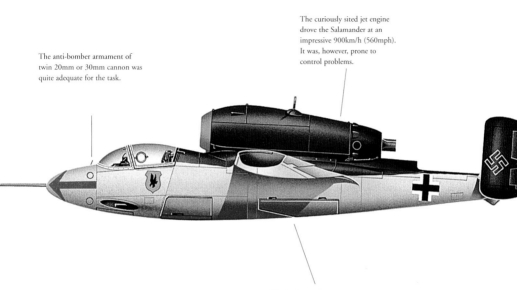

The anti-bomber armament of twin 20mm or 30mm cannon was quite adequate for the task.

The curiously sited jet engine drove the Salamander at an impressive 900km/h (560mph). It was, however, prone to control problems.

The fuselage and most components were made of cheap and readily available materials so that Salamander production did not interrupt other projects.

213

BACHEM NATTER 1945

The Natter was a rocket-propelled interceptor armed with 24 rockets embedded in the nose. These were covered by a temporary cap to improve aerodynamic performance. The pilot would simply point the plane at a target and trigger the rockets, which fired all at once like a shotgun shell. Afterwards, the pilot escaped by jettisoning the entire front end of the aircraft and deploying a parachute from the rear, slowing the craft and effectively flinging him out. He then parachuted back to Earth.

The Bachem Natter never flew in combat, so its effectiveness cannot be properly determined. It is not likely to have been very great.

SPECIFICATIONS

TYPE:	Disposable interceptor
CREW:	1
ARMAMENT:	24 x 73mm or 55mm anti-aircraft rocket
RANGE:	60km (37 miles)
SPEED:	1000km/h (620mph)
COMBAT CEILING:	9,000m+ (29,500ft+)
USERS:	Germany

A Natter with the nose cone removed to show its armament of air-to-air rockets. These were theoretically powerful enough to down a bomber and were used like a scattergun in the hope that there was a target somewhere within the area that the salvo passed through.

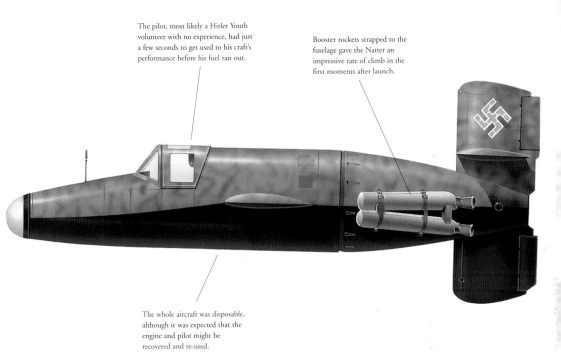

The pilot, most likely a Hitler Youth volunteer with no experience, had just a few seconds to get used to his craft's performance before his fuel ran out.

Booster rockets strapped to the fuselage gave the Natter an impressive rate of climb in the first moments after launch.

The whole aircraft was disposable, although it was expected that the engine and pilot might be recovered and re-used.

VOUGHT F7U CUTLASS 1948

The main fault with the Cutlass was a severe lack of thrust. Its engines needed a lot of maintenance and sometimes failed anyway. The Cutlass could not land safely on one engine, so regulations called for the pilot to eject near the carrier, rather than attempt a single-engined approach.

The Cutlass's guns were mounted above the air intakes and could cause the engines to flame out or even suffer critical damage. Several aircraft were lost due to their own weapons. On top of all that, the Cutlass suffered from weak landing gear, which sometimes collapsed on an arrested landing. This usually killed the pilot.

SPECIFICATIONS

TYPE:	Naval fighter
CREW:	1
ARMAMENT:	4 x 20mm cannon
RANGE:	750km (466 miles)
SPEED:	1100km/h (683mph)
COMBAT CEILING:	14,000m (46,000ft)
USERS:	USA

A Vought Cutlass takes off from a carrier. The Cutlass was in many ways an innovative aircraft and may have been an attempt to do too much at once. It had good flying characteristics when its engines were working properly, but unfortunately failures were far too common.

A landing-gear failure would bring the long nose crashing down to a carrier deck when the arrester hook caught, with serious consequences for pilot and plane.

The Cutlass's engines were prone to failure even when properly maintained. It was too underpowered to land safely on one engine.

Despite its flaws, the Cutlass was overall a good aircraft and pleasant to fly. If the engine problems had been fixed it might have been a world-beater.

SUPERMARINE SWIFT 1950

An early jet fighter mounting 30mm cannon and featuring swept wings and tailplane, the Swift suffered from an alarming tendency to pitch up and try to flip over in flight. This was fixed by ballasting the nose, reducing performance accordingly. Much experimentation later, a new tailplane apparently did away with the problem for good. This was disproved when two aircraft were lost by the RAF as a result of pitch-up incidents. On top of all this, the reheat (afterburner) feature of the Swift F4 version did not work at high altitude, which in a high-level interceptor was a serious flaw.

SPECIFICATIONS

TYPE:	Air-superiority fighter
CREW:	1
ARMAMENT:	4 x 30mm cannon
RANGE:	1000km (620 miles)
SPEED:	1150km/h (714mph)
COMBAT CEILING:	14,000m (46,000ft)
USERS:	Britain

The Swift suffered mainly from being developed too fast and rushed into production. It was needed in service and corners were cut accordingly. After much in-service development, the Swift emerged as a decent fighter, but by then it was doomed to rapid replacement.

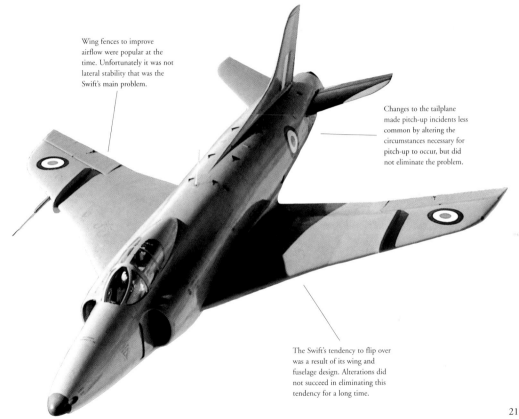

Wing fences to improve airflow were popular at the time. Unfortunately it was not lateral stability that was the Swift's main problem.

Changes to the tailplane made pitch-up incidents less common by altering the circumstances necessary for pitch-up to occur, but did not eliminate the problem.

The Swift's tendency to flip over was a result of its wing and fuselage design. Alterations did not succeed in eliminating this tendency for a long time.

219

NB-36H NUCLEAR-POWERED BOMBER 1951

Conceived in 1946, this long-running project could actually have produced an aircraft powered by an onboard nuclear reactor. It was found that to avoid radiation interfering with the instruments (and the crew), a four-ton lead shield between cockpit and reactor was necessary, along with foot-thick leaded cockpit glass. The recoil from its defensive armament sometimes caused onboard electronics to malfunction.

The plane flew with a reactor aboard, although it did not provide power for the engines, and experiments seemed successful enough that a version actually powered by its reactor was ordered in 1951. It was never delivered and the project eventually faded away.

SPECIFICATIONS

TYPE:	Strategic bomber
CREW:	15
ARMAMENT:	8 turrets with 2 x 20mm cannon each
RANGE:	5500km (3400 miles)
SPEED:	700km/h (435mph)
PAYLOAD:	39 tons
USERS:	USA

In the early postwar years, everything just had to be atomic. The B-36H was a nuclear-powered bomber designed to deliver nuclear weapons over intercontinental ranges. Its mix of propeller and jet engines could in theory keep it in the air for days.

An NB-36H actually flew with a reactor aboard. It seems likely that had the nuclear-powered version been delivered, it would have flown.

A huge lead disc was installed in the middle of the aircraft to protect the crew from radiation.

The cockpit area was also encased in lead. Much of the reactor's power was necessary to lift the weight of its own shielding.

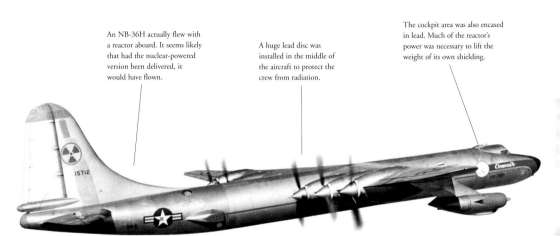

X-3 STILETTO *1952*

Resembling a hypodermic syringe with (rather small) wings, the X-3 was intended to exceed Mach 2 and demonstrate a range of technologies that would be incorporated into a new generation of fighters.

One initial problem was that the X-3 was severely underpowered and very hard to control in flight. Just getting it off the ground was a challenge as its takeoff speed was 280 knots (almost 500km/h [310mph]). In addition the X-3 had a tendency to pitch and yaw when manoeuvring at transonic speeds. All in all, the X-3 was not a success. Despite this, some of its design concepts were used in the F104 Starfighter.

SPECIFICATIONS

TYPE:	Experimental aircraft
CREW:	1
ARMAMENT:	None
RANGE:	1120km/h (696mph)
SPEED:	13,000m (42,650ft)
PAYLOAD:	600kg (1323lb) of instruments
USERS:	USA

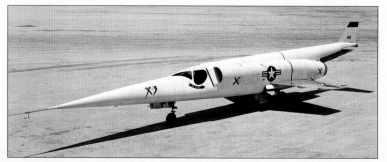

The prototype X-3. Designed as a technology demonstrator, the X-3 was never intended to become a combat aircraft, although this has happened at times. The original F-16 was designed as a technology demonstrator and became one of the best fighters of the era.

The X-3's small control surfaces reduced drag but also stability. The result was a rather unfriendly aircraft.

The tiny wings ensured a very high takeoff and landing speed, creating its own set of dangers and multiplying instability hazards.

The spike-like fuselage was obviously designed for nothing but speed. This represented wasted effort, as the engines were inadequate.

U.S. AIR FORCE

BLUE STREAK 1955

Developed as a means to deliver Britain's nuclear deterrent, Blue Streak suffered from development delays and cost overruns as well as the usual problem facing liquid-fuelled rockets. It could not be kept fuelled and required over 15 minutes to make ready for launch, ruining its credibility as a deterrent, as it could not fire back before being destroyed by a first strike.

Blue Streak was cancelled in favour of Skybolt (which was also cancelled) and was then used as part of a satellite launch system, where it also failed to deliver anything useful and quietly faded into well-deserved obscurity.

SPECIFICATIONS

ROLE:	Nuclear delivery system
TYPE:	Medium-range ballistic missile
RANGE:	3700km (2300 miles)
PAYLOAD:	Nuclear
PROPULSION:	Liquid-fuelled
LAUNCH:	Ground-based silo
USERS:	Britain

A Blue Streak missile ready for launch.
Liquid-fuelled rockets cannot be kept ready
for launch, as the fuel is unstable and
corrosive. Fuelling can be a lengthy process
and this is clearly unacceptable for a
deterrent weapon that must be seen to be
always ready to strike back.

Open facilities such as this one were unlikely to survive an attack. To protect their missiles the British invented the concept of protected silos.

A Blue Streak missile launching on a test range in Australia. Three test launches were successfully carried out.

As a multi-stage Medium-Range Ballistic Missile, Blue Streak had a range of about 3700km (2300 miles).

225

HANDLEY PAGE VICTOR 1957

At some point in development, the Victor nuclear bomber's crew escape capsule was deleted, although the pilot and copilot kept their ejector seats. The crew door was right next to the engine intakes, which made a hurried departure rather dangerous. Development was hampered by the cancellation of the intended engines, necessitating a redesign of the wing to accommodate different ones.

Having finally obtained a working Victor, the British government then cancelled much of its procurement for various reasons, and the surviving Victors were eventually converted to tankers. Ironically, these nuclear bombers have done far greater service in this support role than in their planned offensive capability.

SPECIFICATIONS

TYPE:	Strategic bomber
CREW:	5
DEFENSIVE ARMAMENT:	None
RANGE:	2400km (1,500 miles)
SPEED:	1050km/h (652mph)
PAYLOAD:	18,000kg (39,700lb) bombs
USERS:	Britain

The Victor was designed as a nuclear bomber, but is today famous as a tanker. Victors supported the 'Black Buck' Vulcan bombing raids in 1982, at the time the longest-range bomber attacks ever carried out.

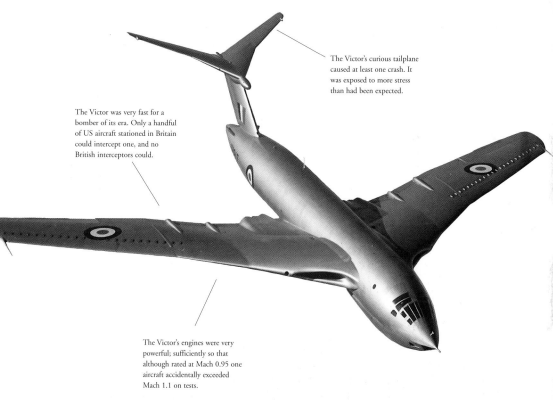

The Victor's curious tailplane caused at least one crash. It was exposed to more stress than had been expected.

The Victor was very fast for a bomber of its era. Only a handful of US aircraft stationed in Britain could intercept one, and no British interceptors could.

The Victor's engines were very powerful; sufficiently so that although rated at Mach 0.95 one aircraft accidentally exceeded Mach 1.1 on tests.

PROJECT PLUTO 1957

Designed to travel at Mach 3 at extremely low level, Project Pluto was a cruise missile powered by an unshielded nuclear reactor that not only leaked radiation but actually shed radioactive debris from its exhaust. Pluto also flew so fast that the pressure wave it created could kill unprotected personnel on the ground below. It would have been able to fly for months and reach any point on the Earth's surface, delivering its cargo of hydrogen bombs when it got there.

Project Pluto was eventually cancelled, which may be just as well. It was not so much poor as horrific, and Pluto is one weapon the world is better off without.

SPECIFICATIONS

TYPE:	Nuclear powered cruise missile
RANGE:	Virtually unlimited
PROPULSION:	Nuclear ramjet
SPEED:	Mach 3
GUIDANCE:	Terrain contour matching
PAYLOAD:	16–24 thermonuclear warheads
USERS:	USA

An impression of Pluto in action. Nowhere would be safe from this terrible device and its nuclear payload. Where a cruise missile can attack one target and is expended in the process, Pluto could attack many sites situated thousands of miles apart, over an interval of days or even weeks.

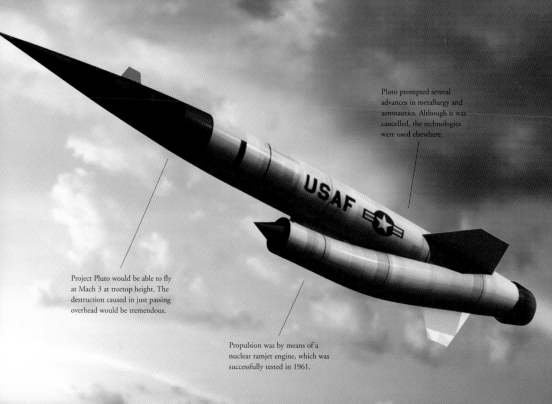

Pluto prompted several advances in metallurgy and aeronautics. Although it was cancelled, the technologies were used elsewhere.

Project Pluto would be able to fly at Mach 3 at treetop height. The destruction caused in just passing overhead would be tremendous.

Propulsion was by means of a nuclear ramjet engine, which was successfully tested in 1961.

LOCKHEED F-104 STARFIGHTER 1958

The Lockheed F-104 Starfighter had extremely short wings and a very narrow fuselage. Capable of almost Mach 2, it was sometimes referred to as a 'missile with a man in it'. Unfortunately the fighter had a high accident rate in service and gained a reputation as a 'flying coffin', with some air forces losing up to half their aircraft in accidents.

One of the main problems with the F-104 was its turn rate. F-104s operated at such speeds that, by the time a target was sighted, it was often impossible to turn fast enough to engage it.

SPECIFICATIONS

TYPE:	Air-superiority fighter
CREW:	1
ARMAMENT:	1 x 20mm Vulcan cannon, 2 Sidewinder missiles
RANGE:	670km (416 miles)
SPEED:	2125km/h (1320mph)
COMBAT CEILING:	15240m (50,000ft)
USERS:	USA, Canada, Germany, Italy, Pakistan, Japan

A pair of Starfighters in close formation. The F104 was phased out in most nations by the mid-1980s, but was retained by the Italian Air Force in a modified configuration for another two decades. It was fast, but had very poor turning performance.

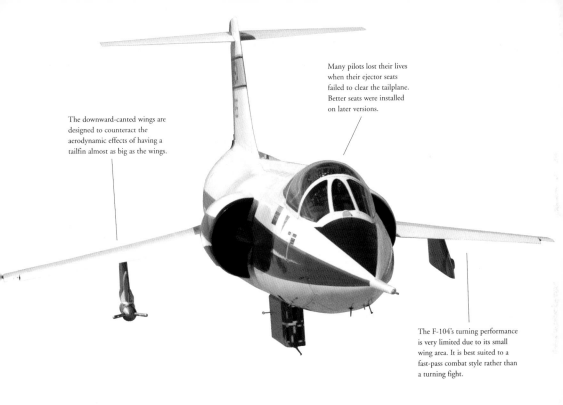

The downward-canted wings are designed to counteract the aerodynamic effects of having a tailfin almost as big as the wings.

Many pilots lost their lives when their ejector seats failed to clear the tailplane. Better seats were installed on later versions.

The F-104's turning performance is very limited due to its small wing area. It is best suited to a fast-pass combat style rather than a turning fight.

AIM-47 FALCON MISSILE 1958

In the late 1950s the United States decided to develop an advanced missile for use aboard its projected Mach 3 interceptor. Falcon was intended to fulfil that requirement. It had a range of more than 200km (124 miles) and a very high speed.

Although the aircraft that was to fire it was cancelled, development on the Falcon continued. A nuclear-tipped version was attempted, although no suitable warhead was forthcoming. The project laboured on, and for a time it seemed that Falcon might arm the interceptor version of the SR71 Blackbird reconnaissance aircraft. This project, too, came to naught. Ultimately, with about 80 missiles built but nothing to fire them from, the project was scrapped.

SPECIFICATIONS

TYPE:	Air-to-air missile
RANGE:	210km (130 miles)
ATTACK MODE:	Active radar homing
WARHEAD:	HE/fragmentation
PROPULSION:	Solid fuel rocket
SPEED:	Mach 6
USERS:	USA

The AIM-47 Falcon was a long-range version of the AIM-4 Falcon designed to arm the new XF-108 interceptor. The aircraft was cancelled and, after being redesignated and considered for use with other proposed aircraft, the long-range Falcon project was cancelled.

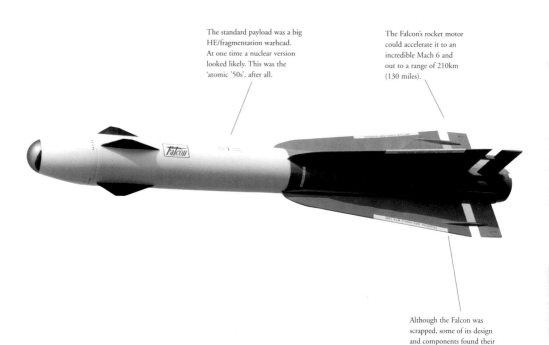

The standard payload was a big HE/fragmentation warhead. At one time a nuclear version looked likely. This was the 'atomic '50s', after all.

The Falcon's rocket motor could accelerate it to an incredible Mach 6 and out to a range of 210km (130 miles).

Although the Falcon was scrapped, some of its design and components found their way into the successful Phoenix missile.

DOUGLAS F6D MISSILEER 1960

The Missileer was a novel solution to the problem of intercepting enemy strike aircraft that might otherwise close with a carrier battle group, launch a salvo of missiles and escape before interceptors could reach firing range.

The Missileer was a three-man 'launch platform' that orbited on station for hours at a time, ready to fire long-range missiles at anything that looked like an anti-shipping strike. It was to mount a powerful radar and the Eagle long-range air-to-air missile, which could carry a nuclear warhead. Problems with the Eagle missile, added to the realization that the Missileer was expensive and limited in application, caused the project to be cancelled.

SPECIFICATIONS

TYPE:	Naval interceptor/missile combination
CREW:	3
ARMAMENT:	6x Eagle air-to-air missiles
PAYLOAD:	HE or W42 tactical nuclear
ENDURANCE:	6 hours
ENGAGEMENT:	185km (115 miles)
RANGE:	n/a
USERS:	USA

The Missileer's armament was to be the Eagle missile, possibly with nuclear warheads. After Eagle was cancelled, the Missileer was more or less doomed.

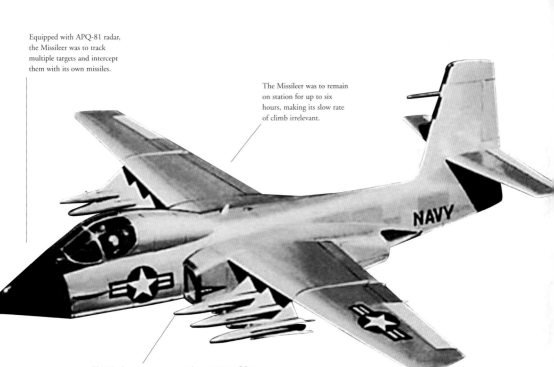

Equipped with APQ-81 radar, the Missileer was to track multiple targets and intercept them with its own missiles.

The Missileer was to remain on station for up to six hours, making its slow rate of climb irrelevant.

The Missileer was in some ways the progenitor of the excellent F-14 Tomcat. The basic idea of a slow-flying missile and radar platform was sound, but deck space aboard a carrier is limited and more generally capable aircraft were considered desirable.

SKYBOLT 1962

The Skybolt missile was intended to allow nuclear missiles to be launched from bombers. This suited both US and British thinking, as it allowed the British V-bomber force to continue having a useful nuclear-deterrent role.

However, actual air-launch trials showed that Skybolt had some problems. Several tests were attempted, all ending in failure. A single missile was successfully launched in 1962, but by then a re-evaluation of the project had suggested that silo- and submarine-launched weapons were more workable and made for a better deterrent. So, Skybolt was consigned to the trash can of history.

SPECIFICATIONS

ROLE:	Nuclear delivery system
TYPE:	Air-launched ballistic missile
RANGE:	1850km (1150 miles)
PAYLOAD:	1.2 MT nuclear
PROPULSION:	Solid-fuelled
LAUNCH:	Airborne (B52 or Vulcan Bomber)
USERS:	Britain, USA

Skybolt was beset with problems, and caused a strain in relations between Britain and the USA. Other British projects were scrapped in favour of Skybolt, and Skybolt was then cancelled at the US end. The resulting political wrangle went on for some time.

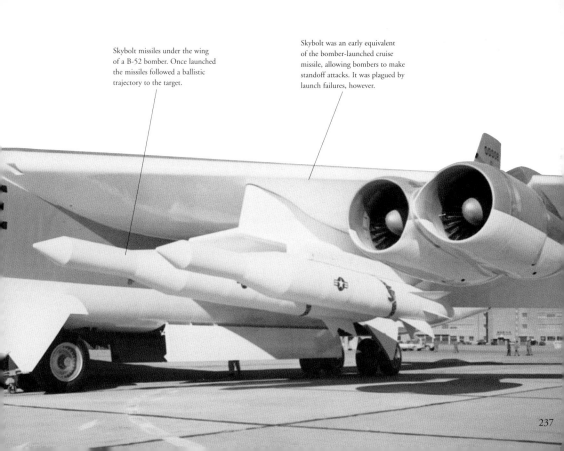

Skybolt missiles under the wing
of a B-52 bomber. Once launched
the missiles followed a ballistic
trajectory to the target.

Skybolt was an early equivalent
of the bomber-launched cruise
missile, allowing bombers to make
standoff attacks. It was plagued by
launch failures, however.

AVRO SHACKLETON AEW 1971

The Shackleton entered service in the early 1950s as a maritime patrol aircraft with a secondary bombing capability. It is probably just as well that it never had to undertake this role in the face of even 1950s-era jet interceptors.

Shackleton crews have remarked that the noise of one taking off is the best sound in the world, because it means you're not on board. Noisy, cold and thoroughly uncomfortable, the Shackleton is not a nice aircraft. The decision to convert twelve of them to airborne early-warning platforms in the 1970s meant that aircrews had to put up with these obsolete aircraft until the 1990s.

SPECIFICATIONS

TYPE:	Airborne early-warning platform
CREW:	10
ARMAMENT:	2 x 20mm cannon, up to 5000kg (11,000lb) of bombs in bomber mode
RANGE:	5850km (3635 miles)
SPEED:	480km/h (298mph)
PAYLOAD:	AEW radar
USERS:	Britain

From the same stable as the excellent Lancaster bomber, the Shackleton's family lineage is obvious – as is its generation. That these aircraft entered service as AEW platforms in the 1970s is curious. That they were still soldiering on in the 1990s is embarrassing.

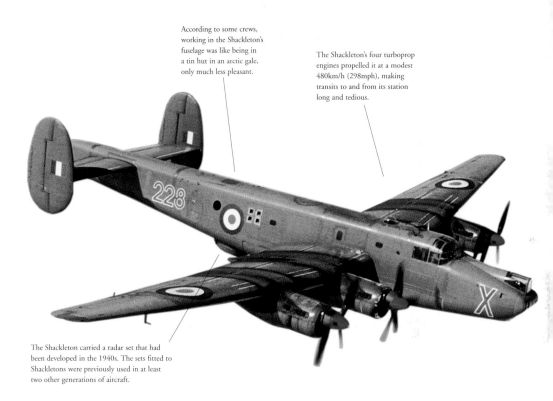

According to some crews, working in the Shackleton's fuselage was like being in a tin hut in a arctic gale, only much less pleasant.

The Shackleton's four turboprop engines propelled it at a modest 480km/h (298mph), making transits to and from its station long and tedious.

The Shackleton carried a radar set that had been developed in the 1940s. The sets fitted to Shackletons were previously used in at least two other generations of aircraft.

BAE NIMROD AEW 1982

In the mid-1970s the British government made the fateful decision not to buy any of the existing Airborne Early Warning systems available. Instead, it was decided to develop a British version based on the Nimrod aircraft.

Problems with creating a suitable radar fit were compounded by trying to jam it into the Nimrod's elderly airframe, and the project was an extremely expensive failure. After spending about £1 billion on development and having nothing much to show for it, the project was cancelled and the E3D was purchased instead. In the meantime, Britain's airborne early-warning system consisted of obsolete radars carried aboard ancient Shackleton aircraft.

SPECIFICATIONS

TYPE:	Airborne early-warning platform
CREW:	12
ARMAMENT:	None
RANGE:	9000km (5600 miles)
SPEED:	926km/h (575mph)
PAYLOAD:	AEW radar
USERS:	Britain

The less-than-elegant lines of the Nimrod AEW patrol variant. Nimrods did sterling service for decades in the anti-submarine and long-range maritime patrol roles. Variants able to launch anti-shipping missiles and even air-to-air missiles have been successful, but the AEW version was an expensive disaster.

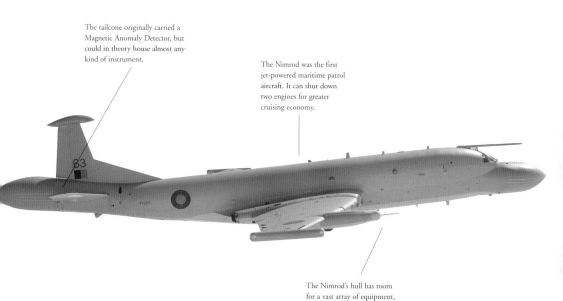

The tailcone originally carried a Magnetic Anomaly Detector, but could in theory house almost any kind of instrument.

The Nimrod was the first jet-powered maritime patrol aircraft. It can shut down two engines for greater cruising economy.

The Nimrod's hull has room for a vast array of equipment, but it was not possible to fit a suitable radar in.

PATRIOT 1984

With its long range and advanced radar, Patriot should provide excellent coverage against a variety of airborne threats. However, like most new systems, Patriot had its problems. One was a software flaw whereby tracking calculations became worse the longer the system had been in operation. Patriot batteries attempted to intercept around 40 SCUD missiles during the 1991 Gulf conflict and there is still doubt about how effective it actually was. One problem was that the Patriot's proximity warhead would be highly effective against aircraft, but might simply chew up the body of a missile, leaving the warhead to travel onward.

SPECIFICATIONS

TYPE:	Anti-aircraft missile system
LAUNCH WEIGHT:	700kg (1543lb)
MISSILE LENGTH:	9.1m (30ft)
MISSILE DIAMETER:	410mm (16in)
EFFECTIVE RANGE:	160km (99 miles)
PAYLOAD:	73kg (161lb) HE/Fragmentation
USERS:	USA and allies

The Patriot missile system had a mixed combat debut, but confidence in it remains high. Large orders have been placed by several nations, including Egypt, Greece, Taiwan and Germany. Attempts to overcome the system's flaws have apparently been successful.

The heart of the Patriot system is the four-missile container launcher which can be truck- or ground-mounted.

Target destruction is by proximity detonation of a fragmentation warhead. This is good against aircraft, but less effective against missiles.

Patriot is guided by a powerful radar and computer suite capable of tracking 100 targets at once.

MV-22 OSPREY *1989*

The Osprey is a tilt-rotor aircraft capable of hovering and taking off/landing like a helicopter, but much faster in level flight. It was intended to replace assault and transport helicopters, and offered many new possibilities.

The Osprey turned out not only to be expensive, but also prone to technical issues. A number of accidents, including a crash in the year 2000 that killed 19 Marines, have cast doubt over the future of this innovative and potentially excellent aircraft. It remains to be seen whether the Osprey will emerge as a viable weapon or be written off as a failure.

SPECIFICATIONS

TYPE:	Tilt-rotor assault transport/multimission aircraft
CREW:	3
ARMAMENT:	None
RANGE:	690km (429 miles)
SPEED:	400km/h (248mph)
PAYLOAD:	Up to 24 troops
USERS:	USA

An MV-22 Osprey on the deck of an Amphibious Assault Ship. The Osprey will give US forces an impressive over-the-beach assault capability if it survives its teething troubles. The ability to sprint ashore yet land vertically in a tight space offers enormous tactical advantages.

The Osprey's powerful engines can be used to hover in place or drive the aircraft at impressive speeds for long distances.

The crew compartment can carry stores, supplies or troops, allowing the Osprey to carry out a range of missions.

Changing from level flight to helicopter mode takes about 12 seconds.

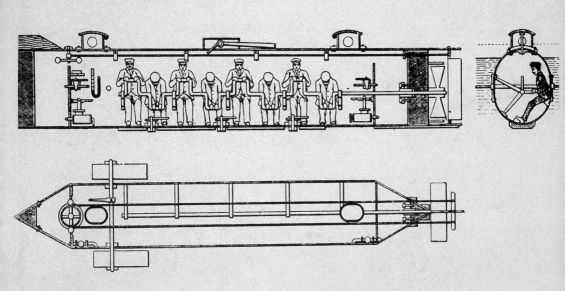

SHIPS AND NAVAL WEAPONS

The naval theatre of war has seen some incredible innovations over the years, and also some very badly flawed concepts. One problem with creating naval weapons is that conflicts involving them are relatively rare. A land-based weapon system can be trialled in a skirmish or a 'brushfire war', but naval systems tend to make their debut amid a major conflict. This is a bad time to discover that the weapon is a flawed concept or simply does not work properly.

Naval warfare can also be somewhat all-or-nothing. An inadequate vehicle or hand weapon will not automatically drown the user and even an aircraft can be crash-landed but failure at sea often means a rapid sinking and very large loss of life. Yet technology is extremely important at sea, so the development of new systems is an exercise in balancing caution against the quest for capability.

Some naval weapons are flawed in concept, others in implementation. Some 'bad' weapons merely failed to match up with the tactics of the day and have perhaps been maligned. And some of course, succeeded despite their drawbacks – usually through the daring and determination of their crews.

Left: *Design schematics for CSS Hunley, a hand-powered submersible which proved less than practical during the American Civil War.*

USS KEOKUK *1861*

In 1861, the main naval threat to the United States came from Confederate ironclads. Various designs were commissioned to deal with them. USS *Keokuk* was one such. It mounted two 280mm guns which traversed inside their armoured housing to shoot from one of three ports.

As well as armoured gun housings and a protected pilothouse, *Keokuk* had hull armour of iron, which was of an experimental design. During action off Charleston, Confederate guns hit her more than 90 times and her armour failed to protect her. *Keokuk* managed to draw off out of range, but was thoroughly riddled above and below the waterline. She later sank.

Resembling a device from a Jules Verne novel, USS Keokuk *under construction. The 1860s were a time of experimentation in which ships armoured with wood, iron and bales of cotton made their debut. Some designs emerged triumphant. Others, quite literally, sank without trace.*

SPECIFICATIONS

TYPE:	Ironclad warship
PROPULSION:	Condensing engines, screw propulsion
SPEED:	16.6km/h (9 knots)
ARMOUR:	Alternate 100mm (4in) iron/25mm (1in) wood strips
ARMAMENT:	2 x 11-inch guns in single housings
DISPLACEMENT:	625 tonnes (689 tons)
USERS:	USA

The low main hull of the *Keokuk* offered a small target to the enemy, but was not very seaworthy.

Steam propulsion drove her at 9 knots in calm water. Being able to move against the wind was a huge advantage in combat.

The two armoured gunhouses protected very large guns capable of shattering most other ships. Their arcs of fire were very limited however.

USS MONITOR *1862*

The armoured ships of the American Civil War were not good vessels by any means. They were incapable of voyaging on the open sea, their steam plants were unreliable, conditions aboard were intolerably hot for the crew and the chances of escaping should the vessel sink were poor. Yet these strange new vessels were able to ram and shoot conventional wooden vessels to destruction without coming to harm. It was quickly found that, bad as these ships were, the only counter to an ironclad was another ironclad, and so a new age of naval warfare began.

SPECIFICATIONS

TYPE:	Ironclad warship
PROPULSION:	Two steam boilers, screw propulsion
SPEED:	14.8km/h (8 knots)
ARMOUR THICKNESS:	200mm (8in)
ARMAMENT:	2 x 11-inch guns in dual turret
DISPLACEMENT:	707 tonnes (780 tons)
USERS:	USA

The turret of USS Monitor *after her classic engagement with CSS* Virginia *(ex USS* Merrimack*). Note the dents where shot had hit the turret without penetrating. The same hit on a wooden ship would cause massive damage. The ability to inflict such punishment without coming to harm was the ironclad's great advantage over wooden ships.*

USS *Monitor's* turret was the only part of her that could be easily targeted. It was heavily armoured and could shoot in any direction.

The broadside armament of CSS *Virginia* offered more firepower, but was fixed to a limited arc. *Virginia* was also a bigger target.

251

CSS HUNLEY *1863*

With no navy to speak of, the Confederate states needed a weapon to allow them to strike at Union vessels blockading their harbours. One idea was an oar-powered submersible vessel which could, in theory, approach an enemy vessel unseen and attach a spar torpedo (basically an explosive charge fixed to the enemy vessel's hull) before retiring.

Built in 1863 from an old boiler, CSS *Hunley* had a crew of nine; eight to crank the propellers and one to steer. Her attack on the USS *Housatonic* was a success in that her target sank, but the *Hunley* was also lost. The age of underwater warfare was off to a shaky start.

SPECIFICATIONS

TYPE:	Primitive submersible
PROPULSION:	Hand-cranked screws
SPEED:	4.6km/h (2.5 knots)
CREW:	9
ARMAMENT:	1 x spar torpedo
DISPLACEMENT:	1.8 tonnes (2 tons)
USERS:	CSA

A pioneer submariner stands proudly with the hand-powered Hunley. *The craft proved deadly to the crew as well as the intended victim of its first attack.*

The hull was improvised from an old steel boiler, offering big advantages over wooden construction.

Access for the crew was via a small hatch. There was no real chance of escape if the vessel foundered.

The vessel was guided using small windows in a tiny pilothouse. Navigation posed something of a problem with such a limited field of vision.

HMS CAPTAIN *1870*

HMS *Captain* was a steam-powered ship mounting four 12-inch guns in two armoured turrets and a good armour belt, a setup usually used by coast defence ships. *Captain*, however, was an ocean-going ship with a full sailing rig.

She performed well in her trials and might have begun a revolution in ship design but for a miscalculation in her design. HMS *Captain* should have had a rather scanty 2.5m (8ft) of freeboard, but due to excess weight her deck was only 2m (6ft 6in) above the water level. This was too little for use in the open sea. *Captain* took her designer and crew down with her in the Bay of Biscay.

SPECIFICATIONS

TYPE:	Ocean-going ironclad warship
PROPULSION:	Twin-screw steam, plus full sailing rig
SPEED:	15km/h (14 knots)
ARMOUR:	100–178mm (4–7in) armour belt
ARMAMENT:	4 x 12-inch guns in dual turrets
DISPLACEMENT:	7068 tonnes (7792 tons)
USERS:	Britain

HMS Captain *struggling against heavy seas in the Bay of Biscay. Armoured ships were considered unseaworthy. It was thought that they possessed too little freeboard to survive any sort of heavy sea. HMS* Captain *proved this theory correct.*

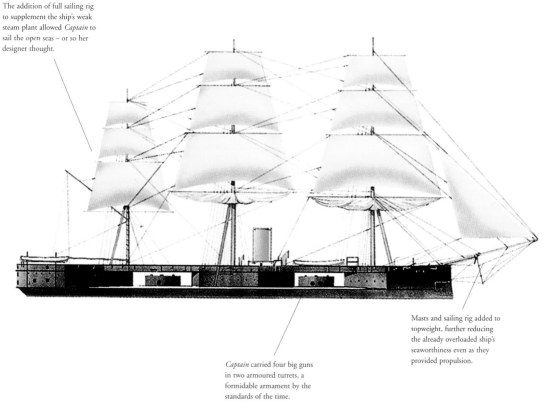

The addition of full sailing rig to supplement the ship's weak steam plant allowed *Captain* to sail the open seas – or so her designer thought.

Masts and sailing rig added to topweight, further reducing the already overloaded ship's seaworthiness even as they provided propulsion.

Captain carried four big guns in two armoured turrets, a formidable armament by the standards of the time.

NOVGOROD 1871

The *Novgorod* was an attempt to create a shallow-draught coast-defence ship armed with heavy guns for the protection of Russia's ports and harbours. Constructed on a circular hull and powered by six engines, *Novgorod* had good armour and the main battery of two 11-inch guns seemed formidable.

However, the vessel was difficult to control and tended to pitch violently in any sort of sea. Firing the guns made the ship rotate, and the vessel was so slow that when operating in a current from astern her rudders ceased to function, causing her to spin out of control. Two examples were built before the project was wisely abandoned.

SPECIFICATIONS

TYPE:	Coastal ironclad warship
PROPULSION:	Six-shaft screw propulsion, 8 boilers
SPEED:	13km/h (7 knots)
AMOUR:	225mm (9in) armour belt
ARMAMENT:	2 x 11-inch guns in single mounts, 2 x four-pdr guns, 2 x 37mm guns
DISPLACEMENT:	2259 tonnes (2491 tons)
USERS:	Russia

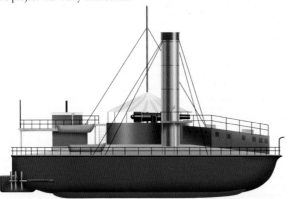

Conceived in an age of innovation, Novgorod was a daring experiment that sadly did not work in practice. The idea of a round ship was not new – many vessels have had a very low length-to-beam ratio over the centuries. Novgorod, however, took this to an extreme.

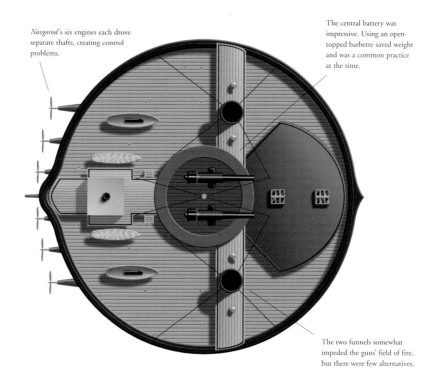

Novgorod's six engines each drove separate shafts, creating control problems.

The central battery was impressive. Using an open-topped barbette saved weight and was a common practice at the time.

The two funnels somewhat impeded the guns' field of fire, but there were few alternatives.

HMS GORGON 1874

With tension rising between Britain and France in 1870, and the French possession of ironclad ships, the Royal Navy put into place a number of hurried projects including HMS *Gorgon*. A turret ship with four 10-inch guns, *Gorgon*, as she entered service in 1874 was a reasonable fighting vessel but a very poor seaboat.

Realizing that *Gorgon* could not function in open waters without meeting the fate of HMS *Captain*, the navy sent her back to the docks in the period 1886–9, from which she emerged somewhat more able to stay afloat. She then served mainly as a tender until being scrapped in 1903.

SPECIFICATIONS

TYPE:	Ironclad coastal warship
PROPULSION:	Twin-screw steam
SPEED:	20km/h (11 knots)
ARMOUR:	203mm (8in) armour belt at thickest points
ARMAMENT:	4 x 10-inch guns in dual turrets
DISPLACEMENT:	3483 tonnes (3480 tons)
USERS:	Britain

In the 1870s the main problem facing navies was that in order to be able to fight effectively a ship had to be too heavily armoured to stay afloat. Whoever managed to create a viable warship that could both float and fight would dominate the seaways, so a rash of experimentation was undertaken, with very mixed results.

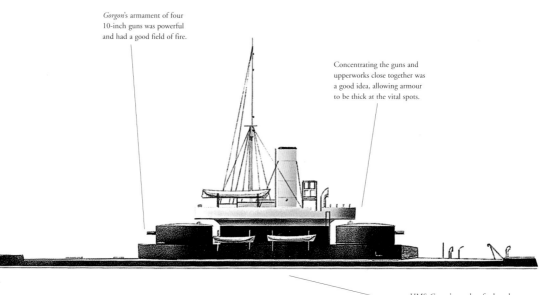

Gorgon's armament of four 10-inch guns was powerful and had a good field of fire.

Concentrating the guns and upperworks close together was a good idea, allowing armour to be thick at the vital spots.

HMS *Gorgon*'s very low freeboard made her a bad seaboat and was a liability in bad weather.

USS MAINE *1889*

A steam-powered ironclad turret ship armed with four 10-inch and six 6-inch guns, USS *Maine* was a powerful asset. She was sent to protect US interests in Cuba, where she exploded and sank. The incident, claimed to be the result of Spanish sabotage, sparked a war between Spain and the United States.

Modern investigation has suggested that USS *Maine* blew up spontaneously as a result of ammunition storage problems or a coal bunker fire. She thus not only scuttled herself, but also caused a needless war, and without even firing a shot.

SPECIFICATIONS

TYPE:	Ocean-going ironclad warship
PROPULSION:	Twin-screw triple expansion engines
SPEED:	30.3km/h (16.4 knots)
ARMOUR:	304mm (12in) armour belt at thickest points
ARMAMENT:	4 x 10-inch guns, 6 x 6-inch guns
DISPLACEMENT:	6513 tonnes (7180 tons)
USERS:	USA

The wreck of USS Maine. *Her demise has been attributed to a spontaneous cordite explosion; an accident that claimed other warships including HMS* Vanguard, *HMS* Bulwark, Kawachi *and* Capitan Prat *in the same general period. At the time there was reason to suspect Spanish sabotage, so this explanation was accepted.*

Guns were directed by officers spotting the fall of shot from the 'fighting tops'.

Warship design in the 1880s was moving towards a more modern 'dreadnought' pattern with turrets on the centreline, but many ships still carried a broadside.

Fire control was confused by a mixed armament of heavy and lighter guns.

HMS INVINCIBLE *1908*

H MS *Invincible* was the world's first battlecruiser. She was fast and very well armed, with eight 12-inch guns in four turrets. This was achieved at the expense of armour protection, but the naval planners had faith that the battlecruiser could outrun a plodding battleship and outgun an armoured cruiser.

At the Battle of Jutland HMS *Invincible* failed to live up to her name when she exploded and sank, taking with her 1026 men. HMS *Queen Mary*, another battlecruiser, did the same a little later, causing the British commander to exclaim that 'there's something wrong with our bloody ships today!'. Fact was, there had always been something badly wrong with them.

SPECIFICATIONS

TYPE:	Battlecruiser
PROPULSION:	4-shaft geared turbines
SPEED:	46km/h (25 knots)
ARMOUR:	152mm (6in) armour belt
ARMAMENT:	8 x 12-inch guns in dual mounts, 16 x 4-inch guns
DISPLACEMENT:	18,234 tonnes (20,100 tons)
USERS:	Britain

The sleek lines of HMS Invincible *and her sisters gave the impression of power and capability. Fast and well armed, these vessels seemed to be an admiral's dream come true. In reality, however, they were simply too fragile for the role they were deployed in, and suffered heavy losses.*

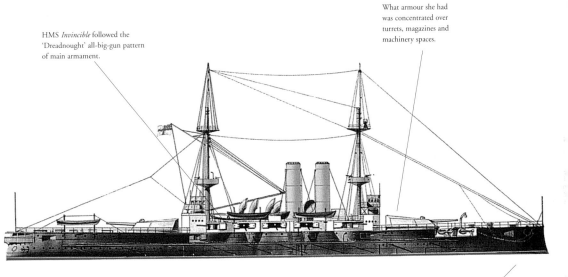

What armour she had was concentrated over turrets, magazines and machinery spaces.

HMS *Invincible* followed the 'Dreadnought' all-big-gun pattern of main armament.

As late as 1908, naval designers thought that ramming was a viable weapon and fitted major warships with a ram bow.

HMS RENOWN *AND* REPULSE *1916*

These two ships were the final British attempt at producing a battlecruiser design. Like others of the type they were fast and well armed, but poorly protected. German battlecruisers tended to carry lighter armament, but be more survivable. British designs attempted to create a battleship without the armour the class needed.

Renown was so lightly built that she could not withstand the recoil of her own 15-inch guns and needed to be beefed up in refits. *Renown* served most of World War II as a carrier escort or protection for convoys. *Repulse* was quickly sunk by Japanese aircraft off Singapore.

SPECIFICATIONS

TYPE:	Battlecruiser
PROPULSION:	4-shaft geared turbines
SPEED:	55km/h (30 knots)
ARMOUR:	152mm (6in) armour belt
ARMAMENT:	6 x 15-inch guns in triple mounts, 17 x 4-inch guns
DISPLACEMENT:	27,986 tonnes (30,850 tons)
USERS:	Britain

These beautiful ships looked great when 'showing the flag', and their massive 15-inch guns were certainly impressive. Indeed, those guns deterred several convoy raids. British battlecruisers, however, were something of a paper tiger – eggshells armed with hammers, and liable to crack their own shells if they used them.

Compared with the lines of HMS *Invincible*, *Repulse* appears to be much more modern. Yet she suffered from the same defects.

Armament was mainly concentrated forward. British ships were expected to steam confidently towards the enemy, not run away from him.

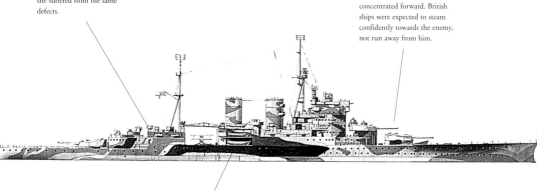

Armour was scanty and offered only minimal protection to even the most vital locations.

K-BOATS 1916

The British steam-powered K-class submarines were fast but virtually uncontrollable, and pitched so violently when diving that the bows could pass crush depth with the stern out of the water. *K26* almost killed King George VI when it dived too steeply and pushed its bows into the seabed – fortunately in shallow water.

Five K-boats were lost, all of them to accidents. The most notorious incident was the 'Battle of May Island' when the flotilla was forced to make a course change and the uncontrollable boats rammed one another during the evasive manoeuvres or when turning back to help. Two boats were lost without any enemy involvement.

SPECIFICATIONS

TYPE:	Fleet submarine
PROPULSION:	Twin-screw steam turbine/electric
SPEED:	43km/h (23 knots) surfaced, 17 km/h (9 knots) submerged
ARMAMENT:	10 x 21-inch torpedo tubes, 3 x 4-inch guns
COMPLEMENT:	50–60
DISPLACEMENT:	1941 tonnes (2140 tons) surfaced, 2512 tonnes (2770 tons) submerged
USERS:	Britain

The K-boats were an appealing idea – submarines that could steam at fleet speed and operate with the battlecruisers – which presented serious engineering challenges. As a result of steam propulsion the class had 'too many damn holes' to close before diving and was prone to malfunction.

The two small funnels were hinged and could fold flat when not needed.

The K-boats were the largest submarines in the world at the time. They were also the worst.

The bulbous bow was fitted to later vessels in the hope of correcting the worst of the boats' suicidal diving characteristics.

HMS FURIOUS, COURAGEOUS *AND* GLORIOUS 1917

These three ships were conceived by 'Jacky' Fisher in his quest for ever-greater speed at the expense of protection or common sense. Laid down as 'large light cruisers' with heavy guns, these vessels had extremely poor protection and after some design changes were eventually built as aircraft carriers. Their lack of protection proved their downfall – *Courageous* was sunk by two torpedoes and *Glorious* by shellfire.

Although Lord Fisher believed in the concept, many of his contemporaries did not. These three vessels were sometimes known as '*Spurious, Curious and Outrageous*', in parody of their names, and it is hard to see what they might have achieved in combat.

SPECIFICATIONS

TYPE:	Large light cruiser,
PROPULSION:	converted to aircraft carrier
	4-shaft turbines
SPEED:	61km/h (33 knots)
ARMOUR:	76mm (3in) armour belt
ARMAMENT:	4 x 15-inch guns in dual
	mounts, 18 x 4-inch guns
DISPLACEMENT:	20,828 tonnes (22,960
	tons)
USERS:	Britain

As conceived, these ships were to use their shallow draught and high speed on Baltic operations. They would probably not have survived long. Finally completed as aircraft carriers, they were altogether more useful to the war effort during World War II, although two of the class were sunk early in the conflict.

The relatively short flight deck was not a problem for the aircraft of the day. HMS *Furious* operated until being decommissioned in 1944. Her sisters were lost in action.

The original cruiser hull form can be clearly seen, with the aircraft carrier conversion perched on top.

As a result of mid-build conversion these ships acquired a rather odd appearance. This did not impair efficiency as aircraft carriers.

M-CLASS SUBMARINES *1917*

The Royal Navy's experiment with big gun-armed submarines was also unsuccessful. Wisely choosing to divert some K-boats that were then building into something more useful (ie anything but a K-boat), the hulls were armed with a single-mount 12-inch gun that could be fired quickly upon surfacing or even from periscope depth.

The M-boats were not a success. The gun had to be reloaded on the surface, negating the stealth advantages of a submarine. In one test an M-boat blew off the front of her gun. The watertight tampion had not been removed from the barrel. Three M-boats were completed, but they never saw combat.

SPECIFICATIONS

TYPE:	Submarine monitor
PROPULSION:	Twin-screw diesel/electric
SPEED:	27km/h (15 knots) surfaced, 16.6 km/h (9 knots) submerged
ARMAMENT:	1 x 12-inch gun, 4 x 21-inch torpedo tubes
COMPLEMENT:	60–70
DISPLACEMENT:	1446 tonnes (1594 tons) surfaced, 1765 tonnes (1946 tons) submerged
USERS:	Britain

The huge gun on this M ('Monitor') class submarine certainly looks impressive, but its performance was limited by the fact that it had to be reloaded while the boat was surfaced. At one time plans existed to make a stealthy approach to an enemy coastline and conduct a heavy-gun bombardment with these boats.

The M-class was fitted with conventional diesel/electric drive rather than the steam plant they would have received if finished as K-boats.

The giant gun was the largest ever shipped by a submarine. It never saw action.

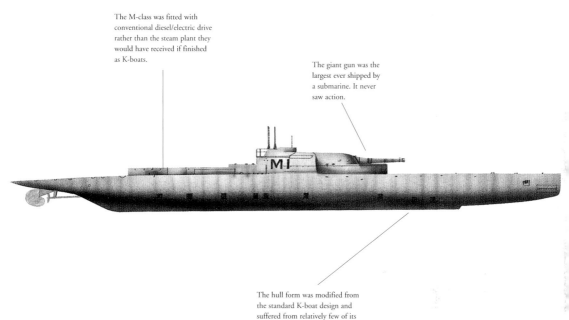

The hull form was modified from the standard K-boat design and suffered from relatively few of its many defects.

HMS HOOD *1918*

Despite the unimpressive performance of battlecruisers in World War I, naval planners liked them so new classes were laid down. First in a new class of four ships (and in the event, the only one built) was HMS *Hood*. She was the largest warship afloat: fast, elegant and well armed.

Although supposedly better protected than her predecessors, HMS *Hood* shared the fate of *Invincible*. Engaged with the *Bismarck* and *Prinz Eugen* she was hit by a shell that penetrated to her magazines. The resulting huge explosion sank her instantly, with only three survivors of her 1477-strong crew.

With eight 15-inch guns, HMS Hood *was able to sink any warship afloat, if she could survive the return fire. She was well liked and respected, and her loss to a single salvo from the* Bismarck *(some have even said that it was an 8-inch shell from* Prinz Eugen *that sank her) was a shock to the entire nation.*

SPECIFICATIONS

TYPE:	Battlecruiser
PROPULSION:	4-shaft geared turbines
SPEED:	59km/h (32 knots)
ARMOUR:	305mm (12in) armour belt
ARMAMENT:	8 x 15-inch guns in dual mounts, 12 x 5.5-inch guns
DISPLACEMENT:	41,004 tonnes (45,200 tons)
USERS:	Britain

HMS *Hood*'s hull form and general lines represent the classic World War II capital ship, even though they were created 20 years before.

Hood 'showed the flag' for Britain many times. It is not hard to see how this beautiful ship impressed allies and potential foes alike with her grace and power.

Hood was inadequately protected against plunging shells, leading to penetration of her forward magazine and her subsequent loss.

USS LEXINGTON *1921*

The general obsession with battlecruisers resulted in the US Navy ordering the *Lexington* class. These were designed as bigger and better cruisers rather than cut-down battleships, but they were still horribly vulnerable to enemy fire.

There were to have been six of these 'fast battle scouts', but by 1921 it was becoming apparent that lightly protected battlecruisers were a liability, so the class was cancelled under the Washington Treaty and two hulls were completed as rather more useful aircraft carriers. Had the design gone ahead, the US Navy would have had to find something to do with a class that was even more lightly protected than HMS *Hood*.

SPECIFICATIONS

TYPE:	Battlecruiser, converted to aircraft carrier
PROPULSION:	4-shaft turbo electric drive
SPEED:	61.4km/h (33.2 knots)
ARMOUR:	178mm (7in) armour belt
ARMAMENT:	8 x 8-inch guns in dual mounts, 12 x 5-inch guns
DISPLACEMENT:	43,272 tonnes (47,700 tons)
USERS:	USA

USS Lexington *under construction, after the decision to complete her as an aircraft carrier. The decision was a good one; it allowed the United States to be seen to give something up under the Washington Treaty and also turned a white elephant into a useful fighting vessel.*

Lexington retained her 'battlecruiser' powerplant and was consequently able to make almost 65km/h (35 knots).

Aircraft complement was about 90 including fighters, reconnaissance and strike aircraft. Numbers varied depending on the mix carried.

US carriers did not have an armoured deck, and at the Battle of the Coral Sea USS *Lexington* was set afire by penetrating bombs. She had to be abandoned and scuttled.

SURCOUF *1929*

The French navy had always liked 'cruiser warfare' or commerce raiding, and designed the *Surcouf* as essentially a submarine cruiser. She was armed with two 8-inch guns, which could quickly come into action after surfacing. The idea seems sound, especially since the low-lying submarine would be hard to locate, let alone hit.

However, after joining the Free French forces with a highly inexperienced crew, she was accidentally rammed by a freighter under mysterious circumstances in the Caribbean. This fascinating ship had no chance to show what she could do in actual combat conditions.

SPECIFICATIONS

TYPE:	Submarine cruiser
PROPULSION:	Twin-screw diesel/electric
SPEED:	33km/h (18 knots) surfaced, 15.7 km/h (8.5 knots) submerged
ARMAMENT:	2 x 8-inch guns, 8 x 21.7-inch torpedo tubes, 4 x 15.75 inch torpedo tubes
COMPLEMENT:	118
DISPLACEMENT:	2948 tonnes (3250 tons) surfaced, 3904 tonnes (4304 tons) submerged
USERS:	France

Surcouf *in port. One of just a handful of big-gun submarines,* Surcouf *might have made a potent commerce raider or even been able to take on enemy cruisers. Her guns were designed to be brought quickly into action.*

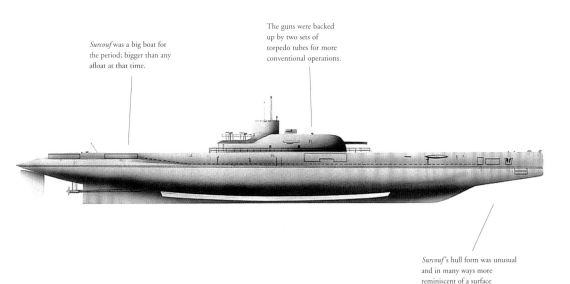

Surcouf was a big boat for the period; bigger than any afloat at that time.

The guns were backed up by two sets of torpedo tubes for more conventional operations.

Surcouf's hull form was unusual and in many ways more reminiscent of a surface warship than a submarine.

YAMATO *AND* MUSASHI *1937*

The greatest battleships ever built, these vast monsters mounted nine 18-inch guns and were designed to resist a one-ton bomb dropped from 4,570m (15,000ft) as well as the fire of weapons comparable to their own. A third ship of the class was converted to a carrier; the fourth was not completed.

By the time they were built the battleship was obsolete. They were both sunk by air attack, although they took some stopping. *Musashi* was hit by between 10 and 19 torpedoes and 17 bombs; *Yamato* by between nine and 13 torpedoes and six bombs. Neither ship was able to justify its enormous cost by actually firing at enemy ships or even bombarding land targets.

SPECIFICATIONS

TYPE:	Superbattleship
PROPULSION:	Quadruple-screw turbines
SPEED:	50km/h (27 knots)
ARMOUR:	9 x 18.1-inch guns,
	12 x 6.1-inch guns,
	12 x 5-inch guns
ARMAMENT:	408mm (16in) belt,
	231mm (9in) deck
DISPLACEMENT:	65,007 tonnes (71,659
	tons)
USERS:	Japan

Both Yamato *and* Musashi *were sunk by air attack. Their impressive protection and defensive armament enabled them to survive for a time, but the day of the battleship was over by the time they put to sea. The age of the aircraft carrier had arrived, and the sinking of these monsters proved it.*

Both ships were built with air attack in mind and had thickly armoured decks. It was not enough to save them.

The immense guns of their primary armament played no part in either ship's fight for survival.

Seven aircraft were carried for reconnaissance purposes. They were launched from catapults located far aft.

BISMARCK *AND* TIRPITZ *1939*

Well protected, fast and armed with powerful weapons, these ships were a potent force but a flawed one. The otherwise excellent fire control system was vulnerable to enemy fire and the deck armour was somewhat thin, creating a vulnerability to plunging fire. Air defences were also inadequate.

However, the real downfall of the class was that they were built at all. The resources poured into these huge units could have been used to build many more light raiders. Although the *Tirpitz* caused a lot of damage by simply existing, neither vessel really achieved anything directly and thus they can be considered a waste of resources.

SPECIFICATIONS

TYPE:	Battleship
PROPULSION:	Triple-shaft geared turbines
SPEED:	54km/h (29 knots)
ARMAMENT:	8 x 15-inch guns,
	12 x 6-inch guns
AIRCRAFT:	6 seaplanes
DISPLACEMENT:	45,498 tonnes (50,153 tons)
USERS:	Germany

These powerful units threatened Allied convoys by their very existence, and thus attracted strenuous attempts to sink them. Tirpitz in particular spent a lot of time hiding in Norwegian fjords trying to survive attacks from the air and less conventional means such as miniature submarines.

Bismarck and *Tirpitz* were 'fast battleships' capable of 54km/h (29 knots), while still able to function as a true capital ships rather than flimsy battlecruisers.

The fire direction system was excellent but rather fragile. It could be knocked out easily, making the ship's guns far less effective.

Eight 15-inch guns was an impressive armament by anyone's standards. It was far more powerful than a raider really needed.

Japanese carrier losses prompted the decision to convert battleships into hybrid battleship/carriers. Both ships of the *Ise* class lost their aft turrets and secondary armament and gained a flight deck and cranes to operate a force of 22 seaplanes.

Flight operations were very slow due to the need to launch with catapults and recover aircraft from the sea using cranes. The flight deck was too short to fly off or recover aircraft conventionally. How much these ships achieved is indicated by the fact that most people have never heard of them. They went into action at the battle of Leyte Gulf without aircraft aboard and were later sunk at their moorings by air attack.

SPECIFICATIONS

TYPE:	Battleship/seaplane carrier
PROPULSION:	Quadruple-screw turbines
SPEED:	42.5km/h (23 knots)
ARMAMENT:	6 x 14-inch guns
AIRCRAFT:	22 seaplanes
DISPLACEMENT:	29.087 tonnes (32,063 tons)
USERS:	Japan

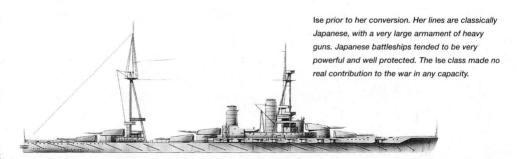

Ise *prior to her conversion. Her lines are classically Japanese, with a very large armament of heavy guns. Japanese battleships tended to be very powerful and well protected. The* Ise *class made no real contribution to the war in any capacity.*

The flight deck replaced the aft armament, but was too short to fly off aircraft, so catapults were used for launch.

Forward of the funnels, the *Ise* class retained its battleship configuration. Lack of aircrew crippled the carrier function, so effectively the conversion just weakened the vessels' combat capability.

The class kept its forward guns, but was never in a position to fight as either battleship or carrier.

SUBMARINE AIRCRAFT CARRIERS 1944

The Imperial Japanese Navy was the only service to consider seriously aircraft-carrying submarines. A class of 19 vessels starting with *I-400* was planned, although only two were built. Each would carry three or four seaplanes for reconnaissance or strike operations. Developing the boats and converting the aircraft was an expensive and slow process.

Along with two smaller aircraft-carrying boats, *I-400* and *I-401* were tasked with an attack on the Panama Canal locks in 1945. Diverted en route to attack Ulithi Atoll, the flotilla lost one boat and had not reached its destination when Japan surrendered. Thus the first, last and only great submarine-launched air raid fizzled out.

SPECIFICATIONS

TYPE:	Submarine aircraft carrier
PROPULSION:	Twin-screw diesel/electric
SPEED:	34.6km/h (18.7 knots) surfaced, 12 km/h (6.5 knots) submerged
ARMAMENT:	8 x 21-inch torpedo tubes, 1 x 5.5-inch gun
AIRCRAFT:	3 seaplanes and parts for a fourth
DISPLACEMENT:	4738 tonnes (5233 tons) surfaced, 5951 tonnes (6560 tons) submerged
USERS:	Japan

Experiments with submarine aircraft carriers were undertaken by many nations, almost always without success. The loss of British submarine M-3 was attributed to water entering its seaplane hangar. The Japanese boats overcame these difficulties in the end, but too late to achieve anything.

I-400 and *I-401* were at the time of their launch the largest submarines in the world. They absorbed vast resources to no real advantage.

Aircraft were carried in watertight hangars on deck and were assembled before flight. A skilled team could ready a plane in a few minutes.

I-400 could perform a conventional attack sub role with her torpedoes and deck gun, using aircraft for reconnaissance.

EXPERIMENTAL HYDROGEN PEROXIDE SUBMARINES 1954

U ntil the advent of nuclear power, submarines could not remain underwater for long, which limited their capabilities. Air-independent propulsion was the goal of many experiments by various navies.

Building on experience gained with captured experimental German U-boats, Britain built two boats, HMS *Excalibur* and HMS *Explorer*, to investigate the possibilities of hydrogen-peroxide propulsion. These boats were indeed very fast underwater, but only at the price of a great many accidents. Their safety record was so bad that they became known as HMS *Excrutiator* and HMS *Exploder*, respectively. Fortunately for all concerned nuclear power solved the problem before a production version was even considered.

Early submarines were basically torpedo boats that could submerge for a short time. Although underwater speed and endurance were improved, the goal of creating true long-duration submarines was not achieved until the advent of nuclear propulsion. Research is still ongoing into alternatives to nuclear power.

SPECIFICATIONS

TYPE:	Experimental attack submarine
PROPULSION:	Twin-screw diesel, hydrogen peroxide
SPEED:	37km/h (20 knots) surfaced, 46km/h (25 knots) submerged
ARMAMENT:	None
AIRCRAFT:	70
DISPLACEMENT:	707 tonnes (780 tons) surfaced, 907 tonnes (1000 tons) submerged
USERS:	Britain

There is nothing unusual about the boats' hull form. Their impressive 46km/h (25 knots) submerged speed was due entirely to their powerful engines.

Both boats were equipped with the most modern escape apparatus possible.

Engine room fires were common, and more than once the boats were swamped with toxic fumes.

USS GRAYBACK *AND* GROWLER *1957*

These two vessels were designed as attack submarines, but were converted to launch the Regulus nuclear missile from a ramp on their decks. The submarine had to surface to launch, and then was required to remain at periscope depth to guide the missile. The short range of the Regulus missile meant that this operation had to be carried out close to the enemy coastline. This was not a survivable mission.

Fortunately, with the advent of better missiles the nuclear deterrent could be carried by boats operating in less hostile waters and these two interim vessels passed into other roles.

SPECIFICATIONS

TYPE:	Missile submarine
PROPULSION:	Twin screws, diesel-electric
SPEED:	37km/h (20 knots) surfaced, 31km/h (17 knots) submerged
ARMAMENT (STRATEGIC):	4 x Regulus cruise missiles
ARMAMENT (ANTISHIP):	8 x 21-inch torpedo tubes
DISPLACEMENT:	2442 tonnes (2670 tons) surfaced, 3311 tonnes (3650 tons) submerged
USERS:	USA

A Regulus missile launch. Operating close inshore with enemy aircraft and ASW vessels homing in on the launch site, the chances of survival after an attack were very small. Former crewmen speak of 'knowing the odds' if they were called upon to carry out their mission.

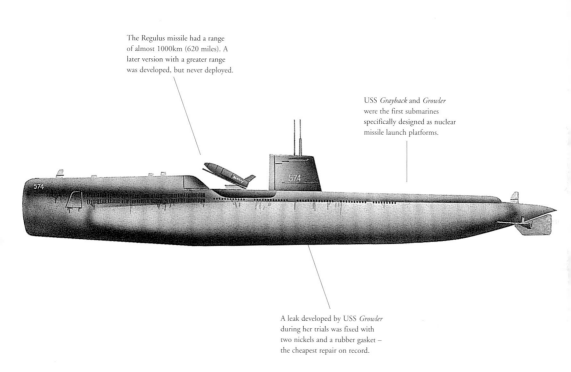

The Regulus missile had a range of almost 1000km (620 miles). A later version with a greater range was developed, but never deployed.

USS *Grayback* and *Growler* were the first submarines specifically designed as nuclear missile launch platforms.

A leak developed by USS *Growler* during her trials was fixed with two nickels and a rubber gasket – the cheapest repair on record.

ECHO-CLASS MISSILE SUBMARINES 1960

An early missile submarine armed with six Shaddock missiles, the Echo class carried its weapons in external tubes, which were elevated for firing. This caused a lot of underwater noise and made the *Echo* class easy to track. Plating over the missile tubes when the boats were converted to the attack role helped somewhat, but the class remained noisy and inefficient.

Several vessels of the *Echo* I and II classes suffered underwater fires or reactor problems – including meltdowns, leaks and other serious incidents – and overall showed a distressing tendency to disable themselves without any need for enemy action.

SPECIFICATIONS

TYPE:	Missile submarine
PROPULSION:	Pressurized water reactor
SPEED:	37km/h (20 knots) surfaced, 52km/h (28 knots) submerged
ARMAMENT (STRATEGIC):	6 x Shaddock cruise missiles,
ARMAMENT (ANTISHIP):	6 x 21-inch torpedo tubes, 2 x 16-inch torpedo tubes
DISPLACEMENT:	4082 tonnes (4500 tons) surfaced, 4989 tonnes (5500 tons) submerged
USERS:	Russia, some overseas buyers

An Echo-class boat on the surface. These boats had a lamentable safety record involving collisions, fires and reactor accidents, and are now all retired. Their noisy hull form meant that the chances of reaching an attack position against a competent naval force were slim at best.

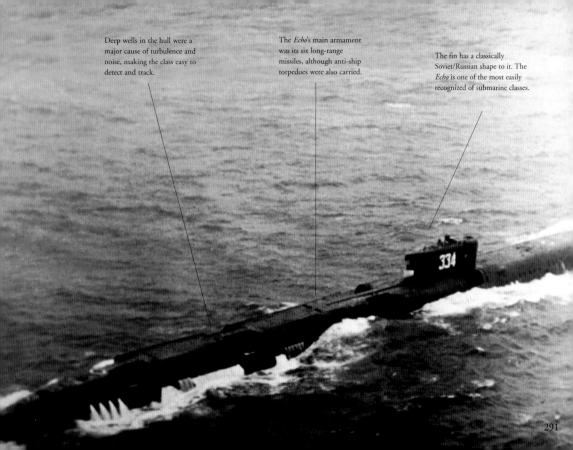

Deep wells in the hull were a major cause of turbulence and noise, making the class easy to detect and track.

The *Echo*'s main armament was its six long-range missiles, although anti-ship torpedoes were also carried.

The fin has a classically Soviet/Russian shape to it. The *Echo* is one of the most easily recognized of submarine classes.

334

MOSKVA CLASS 1962

These vessels were built to hunt and kill US missile submarines, which at the time could only launch their weapons from close to their targets. A combination of cruiser forward and carrier aft, *Moskva* could operate over a dozen anti-submarine helicopters and was a decent surface combatant to boot. By the time she was finished, however, she was obsolete.

As US submarines became capable of launching their weapons from farther out, the ability of the *Moskva*s to counter the threat diminished. Long cruises were a problem due to the poor performance of the class in rough weather and their effectiveness was negligible.

SPECIFICATIONS

TYPE:	Cruiser/helicopter carrier
PROPULSION:	Twin-screw turbines
SPEED:	55km/h (30 knots)
ARMAMENT:	4 x 57mm guns, antisubmarine and anti-air missiles
AIRCRAFT:	18 antisubmarine helicopters
DISPLACEMENT:	13,154 tonnes (14,500 tons)
USERS:	Russia

The distinctive teardrop-shaped hull is clearly visible here. The Moskva class was innovative. Unfortunately the ships were also lousy seaboats and suffered badly in rough seas. The combination combatant/carrier had failed the Japanese in World War II and did not work for the Russians either.

The aft flight deck was a nightmare to use in any sort of seaway due to excessive pitching.

Moskva's 'cruiser' armament included light guns, air-defence missiles and anti-submarine weapons.

Forward of the superstructure, the *Moskva* was essentially an overgrown antisubmarine destroyer.

854

BROADSWORD CLASS FRIGATE 1976

An excellent submarine hunter designed at a time when opposing Soviet submarine forces seemed to be the Royal Navy's destined role, the *Broadsword* or Type 22 Class was not very well suited to doing much else.

In peacetime, warships need to be able to undertake a variety of roles, and with no main gun (the main armament of the Type 22 was four Exocet antiship missiles and of course its antisubmarine armament) the *Broadswords* are limited in this area. Later versions of the class incorporated lessons learned in the Falklands War and, among other things, have a main gun.

The Batch 3 Broadswords incorporated lessons learned in the Falklands conflict, including the need for a warship to mount a main gun of some kind. A class that started life as a specialist sub-hunter ended up as a competent all-round warship.

SPECIFICATIONS

TYPE:	Antisubmarine frigate
PROPULSION:	2-shaft gas turbine
SPEED:	55km/h (30 knots)
ARMAMENT:	4 x Exocet antiship missile,
	2 x 40mm cannon,
	2 x Sea Wolf anti-aircraft
	missile launcher, triple
	antisubmarine torpedo
	launcher
AIRCRAFT:	2 Lynx or 1 Sea King
	helicopter
DISPLACEMENT:	3991 tonnes (4400 tons)
USERS:	Britain

In their specialist area, the early Type 22s were formidable. However, they lacked the all-round capability that a warship needs and were very limited in some areas.

Although anti-air armament was decent, early Broadswords had only four Exocet missiles for surface warfare. It is not feasible to fire a warning shot with a missile.

All Type 22s remaining in Royal Navy service are the Batch 3 version with greater all-round capability. The more limited vessels have been sold off.

F 92

MISCELLANEOUS WEAPONS

Some weapons do not fit into neat categories. Others are simply too bizarre to be listed alongside conventional, if poor, attempts to create a viable weapon system. Some of these weapons are an improvised response to a serious threat, others represent a blue-sky project that might possibly be useful.

As a general rule, weapon systems involving animals are a failure. Even war elephants, which are usually considered to be a viable weapon system, were prone to relatively frequent disasters as the beasts panicked and ran amok. More esoteric ideas like mounting gatling guns on camel-back seem to have been broadly successful despite the possibilities for disaster inherent in them.

This final section is devoted to oddball ideas and deeply flawed projects that wasted a vast amount of time and effort for no useful gain. Like all the other weapons in this book someone, somewhere, thought they were a good idea at the time. Some of them might even be willing to admit to it after the fact.

Left: *Ideas such as dog-guided anti-tank mines could only have been thought up in the desperation of a vicious war.*

FLAMING PIGS *TRADITIONAL*

O ne unconventional attempt to counter enemy war elephants was the flaming pig. The concept was elegantly simple: a group of pigs were coated in flammable tar and, as enemy war elephants approached, set afire and sent at the enemy. The idea was that this would cause panic in their ranks, partly with the sound of their squeals, and partly through fear of the flames.

Perhaps the fire affected their guidance system or the pigs had not been properly briefed, but this porcine forerunner of the antitank missile was not a great success. The pigs tended to run around in a panic and set fire to their own side, as well as disordering formations and generally causing chaos. Their effect on the enemy was negligible.

SPECIFICATIONS

TYPE:	Miscellaneous, anti-elephant
DELIVERY SYSTEM:	Animal
PAYLOAD:	Incendiary
EFFECT:	Psychological
RANGE:	100m (328ft) or less
EFFECTIVENESS:	Negligible
USERS:	Celts, Romans, Greeks, possibly others

Setting fire to an animal and hoping it will flee in the right direction to cause disruption to the enemy seems rather random, not to mention cruel.

War elephants were a serious menace to ancient armies. They frightened horses and were very difficult to stop. They were also notoriously hard to control. It is not hard to see how making the enemy's elephants panic was attractive, although the means chosen seems rather odd.

It should have been obvious that the burning pigs were closer to friendly troops than the enemy, and far more likely to affect them.

THE NAVAL RAM 1860–1910

For about 50 years from 1860 onward, every self-respecting warship had a ram bow, and, it was the ambition of every captain to smash his ship into something. Naval doctrine revolved around the ramming manoeuvre despite the availability of huge guns.

At the Battle of Lissa, fought between the Italian and Austrian navies in 1866, two fleets of ironclads armed with guns and rams met in action. Several ramming attempts were made, most of which were unsuccessful. Only one ship was successfully rammed, and this did not immediately sink her. In the end the battle was decided by gunfire.

SPECIFICATIONS

TYPE:	Warship accessory
DELIVERY SYSTEM:	Steam-driven ship
PAYLOAD:	Percussive/penetrative iron/steel, sometimes iron-covered wood
RANGE:	Contact
EFFECTIVENESS:	Negligible
USERS:	Various worldwide

Against a wooden ship, or a wooden one covered in iron plate, ramming seemed to offer the chance to strike a decisive blow. In restricted waters there was some chance of success, but an enemy able to manoeuvre freely could usually avoid being rammed. More ships were damage by accidental ramming than deliberate attacks.

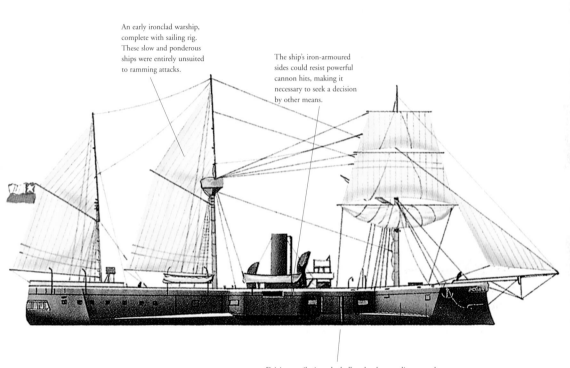

An early ironclad warship, complete with sailing rig. These slow and ponderous ships were entirely unsuited to ramming attacks.

The ship's iron-armoured sides could resist powerful cannon hits, making it necessary to seek a decision by other means.

Driving a spike into the hull under the waterline seemed to offer the chance for a quick sinking. The problem lay in making a clean contact.

DOG MINES *1941*

The Russian Dog Mine was an explosive charge attached to a harness worn by a dog, which had been trained to associate the underside of tanks with food. The dogs would thus run under the enemy vehicles, triggering their explosive payload.

Unfortunately the dogs were just as happy to look for food under Russian tanks as German ones, and if they became frightened by the noise of battle they might run off in a panic, taking live explosive charges with them among friendly troops. When the dog sought cover or simply caught a projection, the charge would detonate exactly as designed – but among friendly forces.

SPECIFICATIONS

TYPE:	Miscellaneous, antitank
DELIVERY SYSTEM:	Animal
PAYLOAD:	High explosive
EFFECT:	Blast
RANGE:	100m (328ft) (contact for detonation)
EFFECTIVENESS:	Negligible
USERS:	Soviet Union

The theory behind the weapon: when the heroic canine defender of the motherland runs under the tank, his explosive payload is triggered, attacking the weak underbody armour of the vehicle in the same manner as an antitank mine.

Vehicle recognition can be a problem for human troops. Hoping that the dogs would do well in their tank recognition training seems a little optimistic.

Animals are afraid of noise, which is in plentiful supply amid a battle. It seems to be a bad idea to have panicked dogs running about with explosives strapped to them.

303

THE MAGINOT LINE *1935*

French military thinking after World War I was very defensive. One result was the Maginot Line, a chain of impressive fortifications along the German border. The Line was a formidable defence, but it did not cover the 'impassable' Ardennes forest or the Belgian frontier. More importantly, it fostered a defensive mindset among French military personnel, which was out of place in 1939.

It has also been suggested that the Maginot Line informed the world that whatever her treaties said, France was going to sit safely behind her fortifications instead of intervening in a crisis. It may thus have encouraged Hitler to attack Poland, with all that ensued.

SPECIFICATIONS

TYPE:	Fortification chain
LOCATION:	French frontier from: Switzerland to Belgium, later extended towards the coast
LENGTH:	Over 300 km (186 miles)
COST:	3 billion francs
MAIN FEATURES:	108 major fortresses
STRONGEST POINTS:	Metz and Alsace
USERS:	France

The fortifications of the Maginot Line were formidable enough. Their German equivalent, the Siegfreid Line, held up the Allies and cost a great many lives to breach. Had Germany attacked the Maginot Line head on, it would have presented a major obstacle and prevented the rapid collapse of France.

The Maginot Line was composed of massive bunkers and artillery emplacements defended by obstacles and lighter weapon positions.

Strongpoints such as this one were designed to support one another and were connected by underground access. They were supplied to hold out alone for long periods even if cut off.

STICKY BOMBS 1940

Attempts to give infantry a useable antitank weapon failed again with the No 74 ST Grenade, a British invention that used an adhesive resin to – theoretically – stick the device to the target, which would usually be an enemy tank.

Sticky bombs tended to stick to the user better than they stuck to enemy tanks. On top of that, they used nitro-glycerine as the explosive component, which was contained in a glass sphere. A sharp blow could break the glass or, more seriously, detonate the explosive inside. The grenade was deemed a failure and issued to Home Guard units as a better-than-nothing weapon.

SPECIFICATIONS

TYPE:	Antitank weapon
PAYLOAD:	600g (21oz) nitroglycerine
FUSE:	5 seconds
DELIVERY:	Thrown by hand
WEIGHT:	1kg (2lb)
FEATURES:	Adhesive coating
USERS:	Britain (Home Guard)

Sticky bombs are mentioned in 1940s US military manuals, along with ways to improvise them in the field. Improvised versions worked no better or worse than the custom-made variety. These weapons were a liability to their users and not much of a threat to the intended target.

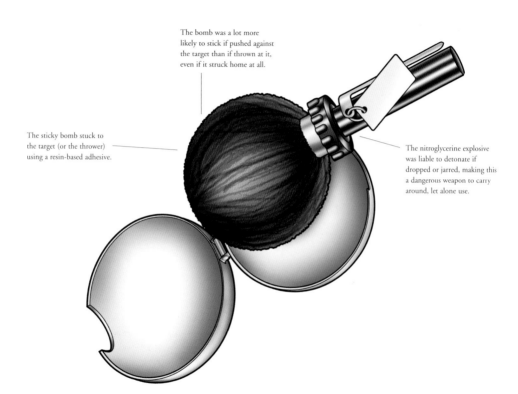

The bomb was a lot more likely to stick if pushed against the target than if thrown at it, even if it struck home at all.

The sticky bomb stuck to the target (or the thrower) using a resin-based adhesive.

The nitroglycerine explosive was liable to detonate if dropped or jarred, making this a dangerous weapon to carry around, let alone use.

THE ATLANTIC WALL *1942*

Hitler described himself as the greatest fortress builder of all time. He was then referring to the Siegfreid Line, or Westwall, that protected the French–German frontier. He also tried to turn Europe into a giant fort with his Atlantic Wall.

Consisting of emplacements, barbed wire, minefields and obstacles including thick concrete walls to prevent tanks getting off the beaches, the Atlantic Wall ran from Spain to Norway and absorbed vast quantities of labour and material. The defences were powerful but very costly, and the Allies breached them anyway. Most of the wall was bypassed and thus fell without ever being attacked.

SPECIFICATIONS

TYPE:	Fortification chain
LOCATION:	European coast from Spain to Norway
MAIN FEATURES:	12,000 bunkers, mined beaches
WEAPONS:	5000 coastal artillery guns, more than 20,000 automatic weapons
INLAND SUPPORT:	Antiglider/paratroop measures
STRONGEST POINTS:	Calais, Channel Islands
USERS:	Germany

The Atlantic Wall included many large coastal gun emplacements, some of them equipped with weapons removed from cancelled warships. A disproportionate amount of materiel went to build defences for the Channel Isles, which were bypassed by the Allies and forced to surrender later.

Concrete emplacements held light anti-personnel and antitank weapons, covered by artillery sited further back.

Vertical walls posed a credible obstacle to tanks; a means had to be found to breach them.

Some bunkers (such as this one) were stormed. Most were bypassed and surrendered, or abandoned without a shot being fired.

THE GREAT PANJANDRUM 1943

The Great Panjandrum was intended to help amphibious forces breach an enemy defensive wall. It consisted of a pair of large wheels joined by an explosive-filled drum. Propelled by rockets mounted on the wheels, the contraption would hurtle at up to 100km/h (60mph) per hour up a beach, hit the wall and blow a hole in it.

The main problem was that the Great Panjandrum had no sense of direction. If any of the rockets failed it would veer off course or roll around in a circle. Sometimes the rockets would come off and fly about at great speed, adding to the general chaos.

SPECIFICATIONS

TYPE:	Breaching charge
PAYLOAD:	2000kg (4,400lb) high explosive
SPEED:	95km/h (59mph)
GUIDANCE:	None
PROPULSION:	Rocket
INITIATION:	Electrical
USERS:	Britain

An illustration of the Panjandrum in action. It could not be made to work as shown here, despite various amendments and experiments, and the idea was eventually dropped.

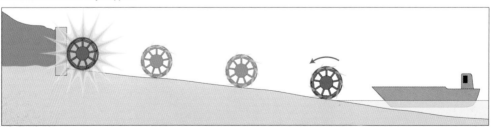

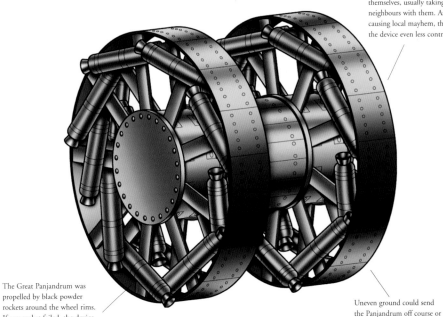

Sometimes rockets would detach themselves, usually taking their neighbours with them. As well as causing local mayhem, this made the device even less controllable.

The Great Panjandrum was propelled by black powder rockets around the wheel rims. If any rocket failed, the device was thrown off course.

Uneven ground could send the Panjandrum off course or cause it to tip up on its side, rendering it immobile.

V2 ROCKET 1944

Hitler was obsessed with superweapons, and although there were some notable successes, many German high-technology projects in World War II were overcomplex and often unsuccessful. A V2 cost much the same as a bomber – and the bomber could be used more than once.

Impossible to intercept due to its high trajectory and speed, and arriving without warning, the V2 was an excellent terror weapon. However, it was

also highly inaccurate – when it launched at all. Many rockets exploded on the pad or turned cartwheels just after launch. These problems were gradually ironed out, but launching V2s remained a fraught business right up to the end of the war.

SPECIFICATIONS

TYPE:	Unguided missile
RANGE:	300km (186 miles)
PAYLOAD:	1000kg (2,200lb) high explosive
FUEL:	Liquid
NUMBER CONSTRUCTED:	More than 6000
NUMBER LAUNCHED:	More than 3100
USERS:	Germany

A V2 ready for launch. V2s armed with high-explosive warheads were terrifying but relatively ineffective, as they tended to plunge into the ground before detonating, reducing their effect. Had they been used with chemical or even nuclear warheads, V2s would have been much more deadly.

The V2 launch gantry was a simple affair. Mobile versions were built and some launches were made form 'field' launching sites.

The V2 itself was a relatively simple single-stage rocket. Development was in its infancy when the war ended; in time ballistic missiles became a major weapon system.

V3 'LONDON GUN' 1944

V3 was the least useful of Hitler's V-weapons. It consisted of a gigantic gun emplacement situated near Calais. There were to be 50 guns, each capable of delivering twelve shells per hour on targets in London and knocking Britain out of the war.

In practice, the shells were unstable in flight and carried too small a charge to be really effective had they reached London, which firing in tests showed they were not capable of doing. The V3's entire contribution to the Nazi

effort came when it fired 44 rounds during the Battle of the Bulge and hurled a few spiteful shots in the direction of Luxembourg.

Part of the V3 weapon's barrel. It was intended to eventually create a 50-barrel 'organ gun' system pumping out five shots per minute between them. This typically grandiose Nazi plan was never completed and the weapon never fired more than a few test shots. A smaller version was built to defend Germany. It failed to do so.

SPECIFICATIONS

TYPE:	Giant artillery piece
CALIBRE:	150mm
BARREL LENGTH:	140m (460ft)
SHELL WEIGHT:	140kg (308lb)
RANGE:	165km (102 miles)
MUZZLE VELOCITY:	1500 m/sec (5,000ft/sec)
USERS:	Germany

Part of the vast concrete bunker system built to house and support the weapon.

Although very tough to crack, these bunkers were vulnerable to air attack with huge 6000kg (13,228lb) Tallboy penetrator bombs. The guns were put out of action by air attack and the complex was later overrun.

GOAT STARING CURRENT?

Some things have to be investigated, just in case someone else gains an advantage from them. A report that a psychic had killed a goat prompted an investigation in the US military into the possible military applications of psychic powers. According to reports, serious research is ongoing into this field, which does indeed involve soldiers determinedly trying to glare livestock to death.

Napoleon laughed at the idea of a ship powered by lighting a fire beneath its decks. Ancient generals would have sneered at the idea of men flying around in machines and attacking one another with self-guided weapons. The concept of directed energy weapons (lasers) or intercontinental missiles bearing the fires of Armageddon would probably have roused Caesar or Alexander to hysterical laughter. It may be that some day our psychic legions will look back on their sceptical rifle-armed ancestors with a mix of pity and amusement at their ignorance. It is, however, somewhat unlikely.

SPECIFICATIONS

TYPE:	Psychic
EFFECTS:	Instant death, information extraction
DELIVERY SYSTEM:	Telepathy
EFFECTIVENESS:	Totally unproven, probably negligible
RATIONALE:	Just in case …
FEATURES:	Extreme 'blue-sky' research
USERS:	USA, possibly others

Many wise people have commented that the most powerful weapon is the human mind. They were probably not expecting to be taken quite so literally.

If the concept can be be proven, then the development of combat capabilities might be very rapid. Psychic interrogation is one potential application, or perhaps the assassination of key enemy personnel at a great distance. The possibilties may be as boundless as our imagination – or just a figment of it.

Just in case there is something in it after all, various militaries have undertaken studies into paranormal combat applications, including the ability to stare a goat (or a person) to death.

Index

Picture Credits

Amber Books: 91, 105, 109, 111, 113, 131, 137, 145, 153, 157, 183, 209
Amber Books/Mark Franklin: 18, 24–27, 78, 80, 81,119, 122, 123, 125, 127, 130, 234, 256, 257, 286, 306, 307, 310, 311
Amber Books/Julian Baker: 40, 52, 53, 86, 94, 95, 298, 299, 302, 303, 316, 317
Art-Tech/Aerospace: 7, 42, 45–47, 49–51, 54–57, 63, 64, 92, 93, 96, 102, 103, 106, 108, 110, 112, 116, 121, 129, 132, 136, 139, 141, 146, 151,

159, 164, 166, 167, 172–181, 184–189, 192–202, 204–207, 210–217, 226, 227, 238, 239, 241, 268, 269, 294–296
Art-Tech/MARS: 14, 32, 33, 67, 90, 142, 155, 170, 171, 218, 219, 237, 315
John Batchelor: 22, 23, 28, 41, 79
Corbis: 8, 10, 16, 17, 70, 82, 83
De Agostini: 255, 259, 263, 265, 271, 277, 282, 289, 301
Defence Visual Information Center: 250, 251

Dryden Flight Research Center: 168, 222, 223, 230, 231
Mary Evans Picture Library: 19, 254, 258
Christopher Foss: 148, 158
Getty Images: 236, 246, 252, 300, 305, 308, 309
Horst Held: 30, 31
Adrian Mann: 228, 229
Richard Stickland: 126, 135
Stock Xchange: 12, 13
The Tank Museum: 97–101, 118, 133
TRH Pictures: 6, 34, 35, 38, 39, 43,

44, 48, 58–62, 65, 66, 68, 69, 71–77, 84, 85, 88, 104, 114, 115, 117, 120, 128, 134, 138, 143, 144, 147, 149, 150, 152, 154, 156, 160-163, 165, 182, 190, 191, 208, 224, 225, 232, 233, 240, 242, 243, 248, 249, 253, 260-262, 264, 266, 267, 270, 272–276, 278-281, 283-285, 287, 288, 290-293, 312–314
United States Air Force: 203, 220, 221, 244, 245